Expert Testimony

A Guide for Expert Witnesses and the Lawyers Who Examine Them

Expert Testimony

A Guide for Expert Witnesses and the Lawyers Who Examine Them

Steven Lubet
Professor of Law
Northwestern University School of Law
Chicago, Illinois

National Institute for Trial Advocacy

Reproduction Permission
National Institute for Trial Advocacy
Notre Dame Law School
Notre Dame, Indiana 46556
(800) 225-6482   Fax (219) 282-1263
E-mail: nita.1@nd.edu   Website: www.nita.org

Lubet, Steven, *Expert Testimony: A Guide for Expert Witnesses and the Lawyers Who Examine Them* (NITA, 1998).

ISBN 1-55681-595-6

Library of Congress Cataloging-in-Publication Data

Lubet, Steven.
    Expert testimony: a guide for expert witnesses and the lawyers
who examine them/Steven Lubet.
        p. cm.
    Includes index.
    ISBN 1-55681-595-6 (pbk.)
    1. Evidence, Expert—United States. I. Title.
KF8961.L8 1998
347.73´67—dc21   98-33936
                    CIP

With deep gratitude for everything that matters most in life,
this book is dedicated to
Doris and Fred Lubet
Hortense Lipton
Noah Lipton זײל

*Key chapters*

— Summary of Contents —

— Table of Contents —

CHAPTER FOUR: DIRECT EXAMINATION

— Acknowledgments —

I am grateful for the thoughtful comments and insights, both specifically and generally, of Barry Alberts, Paul Arntson, Don Beskind, Tony Bocchino, Ken Broun, Robert Burns, Jay Casper, Morgan Cloud, Shari Seidman Diamond, Stephen Gillers, Steven Gold, Janeen Kerper, Susan Koniak, Linda Lipton, Alex Lubet, Dana Lubet, Larry Marshall, Maude Pervere, Lonny Rose, Ronald Rotunda, Jim Seckinger, and M.J. Tocci. I must also acknowledge the practical experience I have gained from working with many outstanding lawyers and experts—too numerous to name individually—on cases and training programs involving the development of expert testimony. In particular, I am indebted to the professionals at Arthur Andersen & Company and Price Waterhouse for their commitment to continuing education and high standards of professionalism in the presentation of expert opinion.

Finally, I am grateful for generous research support from the Morris R. Shapiro Fund, the Stanford Clinton Faculty Fund, and the Class of 1940 Research Fund of the Northwestern University School of Law.

— Chapter One —

INTRODUCTION

A. Who Needs This Book?

This is a book about expert testimony, written largely from the perspective of the witnesses themselves. The purpose of the book is to explore and illuminate the process of providing expert testimony in litigation. The goal of the book is to assist both experts and lawyers in presenting accurate, meaningful information in court.

Whenever an expert testifies, there are invariably two significant impediments to clear communication: (1) direct examination, and (2) cross-examination. Filtered through the awkward and laborious "question and answer" mode, most experts have to struggle through layers of courtroom protocol in order to convey their important points. The direct examination may be tedious, over-long, unfocused, complicated, or imprecise. The cross-examination may be misleading, unfair, obfuscatory, or hostile.

Justice, however, is always better served by clarity. Direct examinations can be made concise and engaging. Cross-examinations can be sharp, even contentious, without becoming unprincipled or deceptive. And even the most belligerent cross-examination can be handled gracefully by an attentive witness. This book, therefore, strives to provide experts with the knowledge they need to overcome the barriers to effective communication in court. At the same time, it may educate lawyers in the proper presentation of expert testimony on direct and, not incidentally, in the most appropriate methods of cross-examination.

Because this is a book about trials, its organization tends to mirror the workings of an adversary proceeding. Subsequent chapters deal with preparation, depositions, direct and cross-examination, and other component parts of a lawsuit. Through it all, however, there is a constant subtext—how to make sure that you get to say what you really mean in court.

B. Expert Testimony

Most witnesses are called to testify in trials because they have seen, heard, or done something relevant to the issues in the case. Such persons are often referred to as ordinary witnesses, lay witnesses, or percipient witnesses. Whatever the term used, the testimony of witnesses is generally limited to those things they have directly observed or experienced, as well as reasonable conclusions that can be drawn on the basis of their sensory perceptions. In short, lay witnesses must testify from personal knowledge, and they usually may not offer opinions.

Expert witnesses constitute an entirely different category. An expert witness is not limited to personal knowledge and may base her testimony on information that was gathered solely for the purpose of testifying in the litigation. Under the proper circumstances an expert witness may offer an opinion on the cause or consequences of occurrences, interpret the actions of other persons, draw conclusions on the basis of circumstances, comment on the likelihood of events, and may even state her beliefs regarding such seemingly nonfactual issues as fault, damage, negligence, avoidability, and the like.

Expert witnesses may be involved in a wide variety of cases. Experts may be retained in commercial cases to interpret complex financial data, in tort cases to explain the nature of injuries, or in criminal cases to translate underworld slang into everyday language. Properly qualified, an expert can be asked to peer into the past, as when an accident reconstructionist re-creates the scene of an automobile collision. Other experts may predict the future, as when an economist projects the expected life earnings of the deceased in a wrongful death case.

In some cases expert testimony is required as a matter of law. In legal or medical malpractice cases, for example, it is usually necessary to call an expert witness in order to establish the relevant standard of care; in narcotics cases the prosecution usually must call a chemist or other expert to prove the substance in question is actually an illegal drug.

It comes as no surprise, therefore, that the use of expert witnesses has become increasingly common in all sorts of litigation. One survey of California civil jury trials, for example, determined that at least one expert testified in 86% of all cases, with two or more opposing experts testifying in 57% of the trials.[1]

---

1. Samuel Gross, *Expert Evidence*, 1991 Wisconsin Law Review 1113.

C. Who Can Testify as an Expert?

There are three principal ways in which experts become involved in litigation. An expert may be retained by one of the parties for the purpose of analyzing information and providing an opinion. An expert may be appointed by the court for the purpose of sorting through conflicting claims or conclusions. Or an expert, such as a treating physician, may be an actual witness to the events at issue.

In federal courts and in most states, opinion testimony may be given by a witness whose "scientific, technical, or other specialized knowledge will assist the trier of fact to understand the evidence or to determine a fact in issue."[2] Thus, there are two threshold questions: (1) Does the witness possess sufficient scientific, technical, or other specialized knowledge, and (2) will that knowledge be helpful to the judge or jury?

The standard is intended to be broadly inclusive, permitting testimony on a wide range of topics. Experts may be drawn from almost any field so long as they can be shown to possess "specialized knowledge." Moreover, specialized knowledge need not come only from education or other training, but may be based exclusively on work experience.

Most experts, it seems, do have academic backgrounds. Physicians, psychologists, economists, accountants, chemists, social workers, engineers, and other frequent witnesses are all qualified, in part, on the basis of their formal education. Other experts, however, such as police officers, fingerprint examiners, or mechanics and electricians, base their testimony on a combination of vocational training and on-the-job experience. Depending on the nature of the case, "specialized knowledge" may originate in virtually any aspect of life. A high school student could testify about teenage slang, a letter carrier could testify about postal delivery, an athlete could testify about sportsmanship.

D. Admissibility

The admissibility of testimony is primarily a question for lawyers and judges. Ordinarily, it is an expert's job to arrive at a reliable opinion, not to worry about the law of evidence. On the other hand, no matter how valid the expert's opinion, it cannot be helpful to the trier of fact if it is ruled inadmissible for technical reasons. Consequently,

---

2.   Rule 702, Federal Rules of Evidence.

it is useful for most witnesses to have some understanding of the relevant tests for admissibility.

1. Area of Expertise

Rule 702 of the Federal Rules of Evidence governs the admissibility of expert testimony in federal courts, and comparable rules have been adopted in many states. Under Rule 702, the United States Supreme Court recently held that it is the job of the trial judge to make a preliminary assessment of the validity, reasoning, and methodology of an expert's opinion.[3] In essence, the judge acts as a gatekeeper, deciding whether the proposed testimony is reliable enough to be helpful to the fact finder. Under this approach, often called the *Daubert* rule after the case in which it was announced, the judge must initially determine whether a novel theory is sufficiently supported to qualify as evidence, or whether it should be dismissed as "junk science." Thus, should an expert's methods or subject matter be seriously challenged, the judge may hold a "*Daubert* hearing" before allowing the expert to proceed.

The *Daubert* rule applies in all federal courts, and it has been followed in a number of state courts as well. Other states, however, continue to follow an older test. Under the so-called *Frye* rule,[4] scientific testimony is admissible only if the witness's tests and procedures have gained "general acceptance" within the relevant scientific or technical community. Under this approach, innovative procedures may not form the basis of expert testimony until they have been adopted, or at least recognized, by a broader scientific community, often interpreted as requiring publication in a peer journal. It is not sufficient for the expert herself, no matter how impressive or persuasive to the court, to vouch for the validity of her own methods.

The two approaches are the most different when it comes to consideration of scientific testimony. In some circumstances, the admissibility of an expert's opinion may hinge on the rule followed in the particular court. The more likely consequence, however, is that experts in "*Frye*" jurisdictions will have to be prepared to explain why their work meets the test of general acceptance.

In any event, it will obviously be useful for the expert to know the specific rule of admissibility ahead of time, if for no other reason than to conform her preparation to the court's expectations.

---

3. *Daubert v. Merrell Dow Pharmaceuticals, Inc.,* 509 U.S. 579 (1993).
4. *Frye v. United States,* 293 F. 1013 (D.C. Cir. 1923).

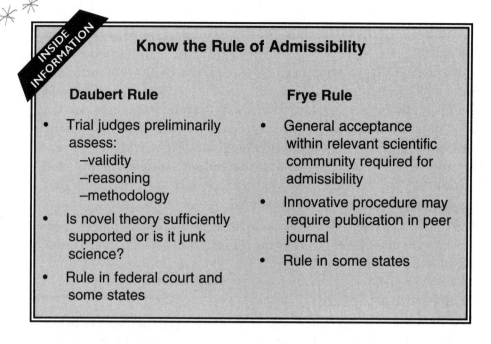

Know the Rule of Admissibility

INSIDE INFORMATION

Daubert Rule

- Trial judges preliminarily assess:
  - –validity
  - –reasoning
  - –methodology
- Is novel theory sufficiently supported or is it junk science?
- Rule in federal court and some states

Frye Rule

- General acceptance within relevant scientific community required for admissibility
- Innovative procedure may require publication in peer journal
- Rule in some states

2. Scope of Opinion

It was once considered improper for an expert to offer an opinion on the "ultimate issue" in the case, as this was regarded as "invading the province of the jury." This restrictive convention often led to extremely elliptical testimony, with the expert testifying to a series of inferences and opinions but not drawing the most obvious factual conclusions. The process was further complicated by the difficulty of determining exactly which issues were "ultimate" and which were not.

Fortunately, the Federal Rules of Evidence now provide that expert testimony, if otherwise admissible, "is not objectionable because it embraces an ultimate issue to be decided by the trier of fact." The only exception is that an expert in a criminal case may not state an opinion as to whether the defendant "did or did not have the mental state or condition constituting an element of the crime charged or a defense thereto."[5]

Judges, to be sure, will often vary in their interpretation of the "ultimate issue" rule. Some courts will allow experts to opine on virtually any issue, including such flat-out case-breakers as whether the defendant in a tax evasion case had unreported income or which parent in a divorce proceeding would provide the most suitable care for the couple's children.

---

5. Rule 704(b), Federal Rules of Evidence.

Other judges draw the line at what they consider to be legal conclusions. So, for example, a medical expert in a malpractice case would no doubt be allowed to state that certain tests were indicated and that the defendant had not performed them. Many judges would also allow the expert to testify that the failure to order the tests fell below the standard of care generally exercised by practitioners in the relevant community. Most judges, though not all, would balk at permitting the expert to testify that the defendant's conduct constituted malpractice, on the theory that malpractice is a legal conclusion that is not within the specialized knowledge of a medical expert.

A competent expert will want to be informed of the court's position on "ultimate issues," since this information is necessary in order to frame the opinion itself.

3. Bases for Opinion

Under the Federal Rules of Evidence, an expert can testify to her opinion with or without explaining the facts or date on which the opinion is based.[6] In theory, an expert, once qualified, could simply state her opinion on direct examination, leaving the cross-examiner to search for its basis.[7] In practice, this approach is rarely, if ever, followed since the expert's opinion could hardly be persuasive until its foundation is explained. The practical effect of the rule, therefore, is to allow the witness to state her opinion at the beginning of the examination, followed by explication, rather than having to set forth all of the data at the outset. It is not uncommon for a direct examination to proceed more or less as follows:

> QUESTION: Do you have an opinion as to the amount of damages suffered by the plaintiff in this case?
>
> ANSWER: Yes, I do.
>
> QUESTION: What is your opinion?
>
> ANSWER: The plaintiff would have realized profits of $4,400,000 over the life of the contract if it had not been terminated by the defendant.
>
> QUESTION: What sorts of documents and materials did you review in reaching your opinion concerning lost profits?

---

6. Rule 705, Federal Rules of Evidence.

7. "The expert may in any event be required to disclose the underlying facts or data on cross-examination." Rule 705, Federal Rules of Evidence.

INTRODUCTION

Under the Federal Rules of Evidence, an expert may testify on the basis of "facts made known to him at or before the hearing."[8] These facts may be provided in a variety of forms. The expert could actually sit through the trial and base an opinion on the testimony of the other witnesses, though most lawyers reject this approach as unnecessarily cumbersome and expensive. The usual alternative is to provide the expert with a body of data before the trial, typically consisting of deposition transcripts, witness statements, source documents, tangible objects, or anything else that the witness might need to reach an opinion. Thus, an economist might premise an opinion on documents such as financial records and department of labor statistics. A psychiatrist, on the other hand, would no doubt conduct a number of clinical interviews as the basis for an expert opinion. A metallurgist could examine a variety of tangible objects, as well as perform a series of laboratory tests. In short, the potential bases for an expert opinion are as many and varied as the possible fields of expertise.

Note that the material utilized by the expert need not be admissible in evidence so long as it is "of a type reasonably relied upon by experts in the particular field."[9] This, however, raises a question. While it is certain that an expert may *rely* upon inadmissible data, it is less clear whether the expert may *recite* the inadmissible data on the stand in support of her testimony.

For example, forensic pathologists regularly rely upon toxicology reports in determining the cause of a death. A pathologist could presumably reach an opinion based on such a report even if it would be "hearsay" if offered at trial. The question, however, is whether the expert, having reviewed and relied on the report, may also testify as to its contents.

The courts are split on this issue. The majority view is that an expert may explain how she reached her opinion, even if this involves relating otherwise inadmissible evidence. Thus, the pathologist in the hypothetical could testify in detail about the contents of the toxicology report. This view is supported by the eminently logical argument that it is meaningless to allow a witness to rely on information and then preclude her from explaining it.

A minority of courts, however, take the position that only independently admissible evidence may be referred to in court. Under this approach our pathologist could state how and why she relied

---

8. Rule 703, Federal Rules of Evidence.
9. Rule 703, Federal Rules of Evidence.

upon the toxicology report, but she could not state or repeat the toxicologist's findings.

Again, the rules of evidence may have an impact on both the expert's testimony and the nature of the underlying work. In jurisdictions following the minority rule, the witness will not be able to refer to the content of any inadmissible documents, objects, or procedures, no matter how essential they might be to an explanation of her opinion. Consequently, the witness and lawyer may want to consider limiting the expert's preparation materials to those that are likely to constitute admissible evidence. In any event, the witness's testimony will have to be structured in such a way as to minimize overt dependence on inadmissible items.

4. Level of Certainty

In most jurisdictions an expert's opinion must be stated, within the standards of the relevant field, "to a reasonable degree of certainty." This requirement may lead to some odd locutions. While "a reasonable degree of medical certainty" rolls easily off the tongue, it sounds clumsy, for example, to say "a reasonable degree of architectural certainty."[10] Many lawyers solve this problem by asking the witness to express an opinion "to a reasonable degree of certainty within your profession or field of study."

However designated, the term is difficult to define. What is a reasonable degree of certainty? How do you know when you have it? Perhaps the best approach is self-referential. Do you, the expert, feel professionally certain that your opinion is correct? Do you have sufficient confidence in your opinion to rely upon it in your own professional activities?

Be aware that "reasonable certainty" is merely the minimum level of confidence required for the expression of an opinion in court. An expert who is more confident need not hesitate to say so.

---

10. Indeed, "a reasonable degree of psychological certainty" turns out to be ambiguous. And some would no doubt argue that "a reasonable degree of economic certainty" is an oxymoron.

— Chapter Two —
CREDIBILITY

A. The Expert as Teacher

For an expert witness, credibility is everything. No matter how well developed the opinion, how rigorous the preparation, how unfailingly accurate the work, it may all go for naught if the expert cannot credibly explain her opinion. Of course, the witness does not want to be believable merely as an exercise in persuasion. Rather, an expert who sincerely believes in the validity of her own opinion certainly also wants to take the time and care to demonstrate precisely why it is correct, and why it should be accepted.

Teachers no doubt provide the best models for expert witnesses. An ineffective teacher will stand before a class asserting that he is smarter than the students and insisting that they write down and remember everything he has to say. Some students are able to learn from such teachers, but many more are bored to distraction. Some students will tune out the lesson, and others may even reject it out of disaffection.

A good teacher, on the other hand, takes care to speak in the student's language. An outstanding teacher is concerned with understanding, not merely the presentation of information. A truly great teacher ensures that the students are following him every step of the way. Thus, the best teachers are appreciated by their students because they make the lessons accessible. Accessible information is credible. And credible information is the most likely to be accepted and believed.

B. The Expert's Overview

No expert's testimony can be truly effective without presenting a viable, coherent theory of the case. It is the theory that provides a framework for the expert's testimony, in turn making that testimony accessible to the fact finder. Without a well-articulated theory, an expert's opinion runs the risk of appearing as nothing more than a collection of technicalities or bald declarations. A theory, however, provides the fact finder with a context for understanding the details of the expert's work.

An expert's theory is an overview or summary of the witness's entire position with regard to the subject matter of the testimony. The theory must not only state a conclusion, but must also explain, in common sense terms, why the expert is correct. Why did she settle upon a certain methodology? Why did she review particular data? Why is her approach reliable? Why is the opposing expert wrong? In other words, the expert witness must present a lucid narrative that provides the fact finder with reasons for accepting the expert's point of view.

The importance of a theory is especially acute in cases involving "dueling experts." It is common for each of the opposing parties in litigation to retain its own expert witnesses. The fact finder is then faced with the task of sorting through the opinion testimony and choosing which witness to believe. It is likely that both experts will be amply qualified, and it is improbable that either will make a glaring error or commit an unpardonable faux pas. The fact finder will therefore be inclined to credit the expert whose theory is most believable.

Consider the following hypothetical case. The plaintiff operated a statewide chain of drive-in restaurants but was put out of business by the defendant's allegedly unfair competition. Assume that a liability judgment has already been entered for the plaintiff and that the court has set the case for trial only on the issue of damages. Each side retained an expert economist who generated a damage model.

Not surprisingly, the plaintiff's expert opined that the restaurants, had they not been put out of business, would have earned millions of dollars over the following five years. The defendant's witness, however, held the view that the stores would have been marginally successful, with total profits amounting to no more than a few hundred thousand dollars. Each witness backed up her opinion with computer printouts, charts, graphs, and pages of calculations. Both used reliable data, and all of their figures were rigorously accurate.

The rival experts reached different conclusions because they followed different routes. The plaintiff's expert calculated lost profits as a function of population growth and driving habits, opining that the revenues at drive-in restaurants would rise in proportion to expected increases in population and miles driven. The defendant's witness, on the other hand, estimated damages on a "profit-per-store" basis, taking the plaintiff's average revenues for the existing restaurants and multiplying them by the number of outlets that the plaintiff planned to build.

Faced with such a discrepancy, the fact finder has little choice but to choose which *theory* to trust. It should be obvious that the simple recitation of methods and figures cannot carry the day. The fact finder, after all, by definition is not an expert and cannot replicate the witnesses' work. Moreover, we have assumed that both experts were meticulously careful within the confines of their respective approaches. Numbers are boring in any event, and the experts are sure to have been equally accurate in their arithmetic. Thus, it is all but inevitable that the fact finder will be more influenced by general approaches of the witnesses, and pay less attention to the minute details.

Accordingly, an expert is more credible when she has a compelling and coherent theory, and when she is able to explain the logic and justification for it. In the above example, then, the plaintiff's expert must demonstrate *why* lost profits can be determined on the basis of population growth. The defendant's expert has to *support* her reliance on profits per store. The prevailing expert will not be the one with the greatest mastery of the details, but rather the one who most successfully conveys the soundness of her theory. The most painstakingly prepared projection of population growth will be meaningless to a fact finder who ultimately decides that only profits per store can provide an accurate assessment of damages.

The importance of theory extends to all types of expert testimony. It is necessary, though not sufficient, for a witness to be thorough, exacting, highly regarded, incisive, honorable, and well-prepared. Her testimony will suffer, however, if she cannot provide an overview that supports her opinion with common sense reasons.

C. Decision Making

To educate people, to bring them around to acceptance of your theory, you must first understand how they make their decisions. Equipped with that knowledge, you may then design your approach to communicate most effectively. For example, you would choose one set of arguments to convince, say, a devotee of astrology, and a markedly different set when speaking to an astronomer, although the language—planets, moons, degrees of rotation—might be strikingly similar.

The decision making of jurors and judges may be divided into two components. First, there is the way that each person makes his or her own choices. This process is highly individualized, some might say idiosyncratic, and far beyond the scope of this book. No expert would ever be expected to look into the hearts and minds of specific jurors and figure out how to speak to each one individually.

On the other hand, it is possible to learn a great deal about the way that people generally go about making choices. Cognition theory has much to say about typical styles and modes of decision making. While it will not be possible to review the entire literature on the subject, the following section can explore some of the more functional aspects of cognition theory.

1. Decision Theory   *Fabulous!*

In decision theory, a "narrative" is a person's mental image or understanding of a certain context or set of events. "Narrative theory" posits that human beings do not evaluate facts in isolation, but rather tend to make sense of new information by fitting each new fact into a preexisting picture. A simple thought experiment can make this concept clearer.

Think about these words and phrases: popcorn, coming attractions, tickets, summer blockbusters. What do you see in your mind? It is extremely likely that you have envisioned an entire movie theater. And not just any movie theater, but probably one that you have attended recently or often. That theater is your narrative. You can "see" the box office, the candy counter, the lobby, the posters. Even if you attempt self-consciously to focus on "popcorn" to the exclusion of the rest of the theater, you will probably envision a particular bucket of popcorn familiar from your past experience.

The essence of narrative theory is that people dislike uncertainty and want to reduce it as quickly as possible. New information is confusing, especially when presented piece by piece, as it is during a trial. Thus, people "call up" narratives as a way to impose order on uncertainty or confusion.

This theoretical insight can be of great practical significance to expert witnesses. Do not expect a fact finder to view facts as discrete units, holding all conclusions in abeyance until all of the information has been fully received. Understand instead that the process of decision making begins immediately, with each fact finder developing a mental picture virtually along with the opening words of the testimony. To be sure, that picture is subject to constant change and refinement as new information is received and initial information is expanded or contradicted. Decision theory, nonetheless, underscores the importance of the expert's overview.

a. Harmonization

A further human tendency is to attempt to harmonize new information with previously envisioned narratives. Thus, new facts will tend to be interpreted as consistent with the narrative, and flatly inconsistent facts will tend to be discredited or rejected. Consequently, an effective expert witness will be the one who can tap into the fact finder's imagination.

Return to the movie theater example. Suppose that someone told you, "I went into the theater and had a snack." Although the type of food was not named, your mind would almost certainly interpret the new information—snack—to be consistent with the old information—movie theater. Therefore, you would probably envision a candy bar, popcorn, or similar movie fare. You would not imagine carrot sticks, cannoli, or stir-fried noodles.

Assume instead that someone said, "I went into a movie theater and changed the oil in my car." You would assume that the person was joking or lying or speaking metaphorically. Your "movie theater" narrative rejects automobile maintenance. Now, there is nothing unusual or undependable about someone recounting the story of an oil change; there is nothing unreliable about the fact itself. Presented in a movie theater context, however, it becomes questionable because it is out of place. In other words, the new information is discredited because it is inconsistent with the established narrative.

Now try one more variation. "I went to the movie theater for a four-star meal." The movie theater narrative would discredit this information unless it was accompanied by an explanation. "It's a new concept—cinema dinner theater." Now the narrative can change; the information has been harmonized.

How might harmonization relate to expert testimony? Imagine that a financial expert is testifying about cost overruns on a construction project. The builder's records were disorganized and poorly coded, making it difficult to know precisely which expenses should be allocated to which tasks. Nonetheless, through the use of generally accepted sampling techniques, the expert was able to make a reliable evaluation. Now consider two different ways to present this information. First,

QUESTION: Did you encounter any difficulties in evaluating the cost overrun?

ANSWER: Yes, I did. The builder's records were an absolute mess. Everything was disorganized, and everything was poorly coded. So I could never really tell which expenses should be allocated to which tasks. That made my job extremely difficult, because I could never be completely certain that I was assigning the numbers to the correct categories.

In this iteration the witness has succeeded admirably in calling up a "chaotic records" narrative. The fact finder's initial template, then, will be that the records were unreliable. Further information will probably be interpreted consistently with this narrative. The examination continues,

QUESTION: Were you able to overcome the difficulties and arrive at an accurate estimate of the overrun?

ANSWER: Yes, it was possible. Using a variety of sampling and validation techniques, I was able to use those records to calculate the overrun. It is common in my profession to encounter sloppy job site records, and we have a number of very good ways of coping with that problem. I am confident in the bottom line of my result.

How will a juror evaluate this testimony? The initial narrative describes an "absolute mess," strongly indicating untrustworthy records. Though the witness continued testifying that she was able to cope with the problem, the general impression remains one of a difficult job with a partial solution.

Now consider the same story with an alternative frame.

QUESTION: What procedure did you use to determine the cost overrun?

ANSWER: I used a standard accounting technique called "sampling." It involves applying reliable statistical methods to a company's records so that we can arrive at a dependable evaluation without looking at every single piece of paper. Virtually no company ever has perfect records, so sampling is employed even on audits of the most well-run corporations.

Now the "chaotic records" narrative has been replaced by a "reliable technique" narrative. The examination continues,

QUESTION: Did you encounter any difficulties in evaluating the cost overrun?

ANSWER: There were no difficulties that could not be overcome through sampling. The builder's records were an absolute mess. Everything was disorganized, and everything was poorly coded. So I could never really tell which expenses should be allocated to which tasks. Sampling is designed for just that situation, so I was able to get a very accurate overall picture. I am confident in the bottom line of my result.

Note how the initial narrative influences the interpretation of the information. In the second example, the "reliable technique" narrative minimized the impact of the poor records. In contrast, the "chaotic records" narrative in the first example serves to undercut the validity of the sampling technique.

The more influential narrative

Of course, harmonization is an ongoing process, and it is not always so simple and predictable as deciding which question to address first. Moreover, a witness at trial will always be subject to cross-examination, in which the opposing counsel can attempt to undermine or counteract any aspect of the direct testimony.

Nonetheless, it is useful to understand that judges and juries engage in a constant process of harmonization. Once a narrative has been adopted they will tend to interpret new information in light of that framework until they have been persuaded or educated to do otherwise. Take heed: Just as it is harder to change someone's mind than it is to make an initial impression, it is harder to change a narrative than to invoke one in the first place.

b. Gaps

All narratives have gaps. It is humanly impossible to tell a story that contains all of the details that one might observe in daily life. Consequently, all testimony has gaps. The introduction of evidence is limited by the rules of admissibility and the endurance of the fact finder to a minute fraction of what the witness really saw, did, or considered. This must be so lest the trial of even the simplest case go on forever, eventually outlasting even the most determined juror's capacity to hear and comprehend.

But the existence of gaps in the evidence does not mean that there will be gaps in the fact finder's understanding. Instead, narrative theory informs us that many of the gaps will be filled by the fact finder's reconstruction (some would say imagination). As a witness, you have more or less active control over the information that you present. As a witness, you can state your overview, give your opinions, and present the data in support of your conclusions. Whenever you leave out a detail, however, the void may well be filled—consistent with a narrative—by the fact finder's own supposition. This is a process over which you have little or no control.

Consider the presentation of a simple story. "I went to a racetrack to see the ponies run. I made a few bets, but I didn't win a single one, so I had a drink and went home." This account has more gaps than it has information. Many of them will be filled in by the reader who may, among other things, imagine the number of horses, the color of their silks, the distance from the track to the grandstand, the crowd along the rail, the lines at the betting windows, and all manner of other obvious details. If those details are inconsequential to the story, then there is no risk in leaving them out. Let the reader imagine them however he wishes.

On the other hand, suppose that a detail is potentially important. Suppose that the storyteller truly cares about one of the elements. Suddenly, there is great cost in leaving it out. Return to the racetrack story. The relater of the story mentions having a "drink." What does your experience tell you about people's drinking habits at racetracks? Beer? Whiskey? Diet soda? Lemonade? Whatever the beverage, it is almost certain that the gap will be filled. And if the story is being told in a trial, the nature of the drink might matter very much.

It is easy to understand the significance of gaps in a narrative story such as eyewitness testimony, but they occur in expert testimony as well. Imagine a trial over insurance coverage for a building fire. The insurance company, claiming that the loss was caused by arson, called the municipal fire chief as an expert witness. In response, the policyholder called a private fire investigator as an expert witness. The investigator testified convincingly about her education, training, and background. She recounted her extensive site visits and laboratory analysis. Concluding that the fire was caused accidentally, she presented rigorous proof of her position. The witness, however, said nothing about how she came to be retained by the building owner.

The expert's retention is now a gap. Whether or not addressed by the testimony, the trier of fact may fill in that gap by reference to an imagined narrative. But most people probably have almost no actual experience with private fire investigators, so what sort of narrative will it be? A gumshoe-private-detective narrative? An ivory-tower, white-lab-coat narrative? A bought-and-paid-for-mouthpiece narrative? The answer, of course, cannot be known. The only certainty is that the jurors have been given free rein to imagine all sorts of scenarios, none of which may be accurate, but any one of which may seriously affect the reception of the expert's testimony.

The lesson here is that the absence of evidence is not the same as the absence of information. It is only the absence of explicitly spoken information. Do not assume that the fact finder is not thinking about something, or even relying on it, simply because it was not addressed in the testimony. Of course, no expert can testify in an actual trial without leaving gaps. That would be impossible to do and unbearable to attempt. Instead, the challenge is to evaluate the significance of the gaps and fill in the important ones.

A point especially for the lawyer.

2. Story Framing

Decision theory does nothing more than provide us with a positive description of how people tend to think and decide. It is not a means of subliminal manipulation, nor is it a magic key that allows lawyers and witnesses access to a fact finder's innermost motivations. It may be best to think of decision theory as providing a sort of language, an approach that allows an expert to address the fact finder in terms that are most likely to be understood.

The most important thing to know about narrative theory is that it exists. The second most important thing is that narratives are far from immutable. People can reject or abandon narratives just as they can change their minds about other matters. The simplest way to neutralize a narrative is with a counternarrative—a different and equally compelling context into which the fact finder can fit the trial's information.

This can often be accomplished through "story framing," or connecting a witness's theory to a familiar narrative structure. Imagine that you are the "cost overrun" expert from the earlier example and that the opposing attorney in the case has convincingly established a "chaotic records" narrative. You hope that the jury can understand that the poor records do not really undermine the accuracy of your opinion. You could, of course, flatly deny all of the negative implications: construction records are often poorly kept, accountants work with such records all of the time, many successful businesses rely on sampling for their internal audits and other important accounting decisions. But the harmonization principle tells us that such new information—by now inconsistent with the established narrative—stands a good chance of being rejected.

Story framing allows a different approach. Instead of arguing about the usefulness of accounting techniques, the witness can suggest an alternative narrative that will be more familiar and comprehensible than the "chaotic records" narrative. What would constitute an "adequate records" framework? If the facts support it, perhaps you could structure your testimony around the idea that you are a reconstructionist or rebuilder. Everybody understands the concept of repair. Damaged automobiles can be mended in a body shop by a mechanic with the proper parts and tools. Archeologists reconstruct buildings that collapsed in ruins ages in the past. Parents restore children's rooms to order, despite the most alarming jumble of clothes, books, and personal effects.

The point is that the world is filled with people who regularly bring order to chaos. It is not an unusual sort of occupation, and it can be done safely, effectively, and reliably. Within that framework, the accountant's use of construction records becomes far more understandable.

D. Credibility Variables

A number of variables in presentation have been found to affect credibility, either positively or negatively.

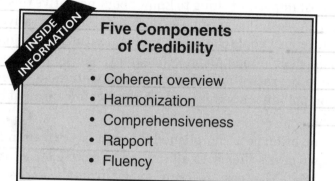

INSIDE INFORMATION

Five Components of Credibility

- Coherent overview
- Harmonization
- Comprehensiveness
- Rapport
- Fluency

1. Rapport

Rapport exercises a strongly positive influence on credibility. All things being equal, a fact finder will be more open to the position of someone who is likable, engaging, interested, committed, and lively. These factors are more or less within the control of the expert, though they should never be overdone. A genuine effort to communicate, and reasonable enthusiasm about the subject matter, will always be appreciated. Insincerity, however, is deadly.

Perhaps the single most important aspect of rapport is direct communication. Because trials are conducted in question-and-answer format, it is very easy for the examination of an expert to take on the appearance of a private conversation between the witness and counsel. There is never a good reason to shut out the fact finder. A competent expert will understand that the questions may come from the lawyer, but that the answers must be given for the benefit of the judge or jury.

Sadly, the rapport phenomenon also has its downside. Studies have indicated that jurors are somewhat more likely to credit the testimony of witnesses who are tall, attractive, and "demographically similar" to the jurors themselves. Fortunately, these biases are usually unconscious and can often be neutralized through skillful, rapport-building testimony.

2. Reporting Bias

The appearance of self-interest tends to negate credibility. Conversely, a communicator is more likely to be believed when contradicting apparent self-interest.

Expert witnesses should be keenly aware of this phenomenon. Nothing will undercut a witness's credibility more quickly than assuming the demeanor of an adversary. Of course, a witness will want to stand behind and defend her opinion. A witness might even be appropriately seen as an advocate for certain positions or beliefs. For example, a psychologist might truly believe that young children should not be separated from their parents, except in the most compelling circumstances. Testifying in a child custody case, it would not undermine the expert's credibility to be regarded as an advocate for parental rights or family unity.

On the other hand, the witness would be damaged if she crossed the line from advocating her own opinion to advocating a particular litigant's cause. At that moment, the witness becomes an adversary, a party who expresses a self-interest in the outcome of the case. Here is the distinction: The witness may believe that children should not be removed from their parents except in the most compelling circumstances and may advocate that position to the court. The witness may believe that the circumstances of the current case are not sufficiently compelling, and she may advocate that opinion to the court. Now, imagine the following question to the witness:

QUESTION: If the situation were more drastic, wouldn't it be in this child's interest to be removed from this family?

Under the adversary system, a *lawyer* for the family would always have to find a way to give a negative answer, because an adversary is dedicated to the goals of the client. A witness, however, ultimately cannot be swayed by the outcome of the case or the interests of the client. To avoid becoming an adversary, then, the witness in the above example must agree without quibbling—in a drastic situation it would be in this child's interest to be removed from this family.

This brings up three further points on reporting bias. First, credibility suffers when an expert refuses to make an obvious concession. Not only will the fact finder be unlikely to believe the specific denial, but the apparent reporting bias of the witness may taint everything else she has to say.

Making concessions a difficult area.

As a corollary, credibility is enhanced by a candid willingness to make concessions. No case is perfect and no opinion is airtight. An objective expert should be willing to look at both sides of the story, so reporting bias is therefore negated when a witness is willing to agree with certain points raised by the other side.

Which brings us to the final point. Concessions are usually taken very seriously by the fact finder and may often be given evidentiary weight out of proportion to their true significance. They should not be made lightly or carelessly; an unthinking concession may needlessly undermine even the most rigorous opinion.

3. Knowledge Bias

A demonstrable command of relevant information correlates strongly with credibility. The appearance of limited knowledge tends to diminish credibility.

For an expert witness, this insight means only one thing: Be prepared. Solid preparation is intrinsically valuable, and it is also an important tool in establishing trust. Recall that an expert witness is a teacher. Good teachers are expected to be masters of their subject matter, able to answer pertinent questions as they arise.

On direct examination, a witness's testimony may be bolstered by showing that he knows all that he ought to know. For example, the police officer who investigated an automobile accident might be asked to give a detailed description of the surrounding intersection, even if that information is not strictly relevant to his conclusions about the cause of the collision.

By the same token, cross-examination might be used to emphasize a witness's lack of knowledge in circumstances where he would be expected to know the answers. Thus, the accident investigator could be asked about something like weekly traffic patterns. Though the daily traffic flow might have little bearing on the cause of a specific accident, the implication would be "If he doesn't know that, what else doesn't he know?"

4. Fluency

Fluency adds to credibility. Ease of communication, visible comfort level, the ability to speak without stammering or pausing—all of these seem to create an appearance of knowledge and reliability. Interestingly, a number of studies have concluded that rapid speaking (to a point) tends to increase believability. This seems counterintuitive given the generally poor reputation of the "fast-talking salesman," and there certainly must be substantial regional variation in the way that rapid speaking is received. No doubt, unnaturally slow speech is generally taken as an indicator of uncertainty or worse. As pace increases it will eventually reach an optimum level—fast enough to be reassuring but not so fast as to seem slick or devious.

5. Language of Expression

There is a tradition in many scholarly and technical fields of hedging or qualifying the language in which opinions are expressed. This makes great sense when discussing research, since conclusions are always tentative and results are always subject to further inquiry. Thus, it is not uncommon for professionals to use terms such as "to the best of my current understanding" or "as far as we can tell." While this language is meant to convey open-mindedness as opposed to uncertainty, it can be damaging to a witness's credibility in the courtroom. To prevent inadvertent miscommunication, expert witnesses should attempt to testify in straightforward, decisive terms that emphasize the witness's accuracy and certainty.

Language is often most expressive when making use of nouns and verbs. This may seem counterintuitive; many lawyers and witnesses think that adjectives are the best words for drawing a mental image. But the fact is that adjectives tend to convey judgments, which can make them argumentative, which can make them seem undependable. Nouns and verbs, however, suggest not a belief about something but rather the thing itself.

Consider this example. Suppose that someone told you that a certain automobile was "ugly." The adjective "ugly" conveys an aesthetic judgment. Depending upon the speaker and the circumstances, you might agree with the characterization and you might not. Adding an adverb does not help. The car was *really* ugly. The car was *incredibly* ugly. Even with inflection, adjectives and adverbs simply tend to lack intrinsically descriptive power. They convey opinions, but not the basis for the opinions.

Now suppose that the same person told you that the automobile's paint had peeled off of the doors and that its hood was so rusted that you could see right through to the engine in several places. The windshield was covered by a spiderweb of fracture lines. The tailpipe dragged on the ground. One fender was missing, and another was replaced by a mismatched part from a different model. The hubcaps were gone, and the trunk was held down with bungee cords.

It should be apparent that the nouns and verbs tell a powerful story—that car was ugly.

E. Appearance and Demeanor

Fact finders unfailingly believe that they can determine the truthfulness of a witness based upon the person's appearance and demeanor in the courtroom. In fact, this principle is all but enshrined in procedural law, which prevents appellate courts from second-guessing a trial judge or jury's superior opportunity to observe the witness.

It is somewhat disquieting, therefore, to realize that much research indicates an extremely high error rate in distinguishing truth from deceit. Studies have consistently found that observers are wrong between thirty and sixty percent of the time when determining whether a witness is telling the truth or lying. Interesting, it appears that almost no profession does better than any other when it comes to accurately evaluating the truthfulness of others. Judges, police officers, social workers, and psychiatrists all tended to score in the same overall range as the general population. Nonetheless, people express great certainty in the belief that verbal and nonverbal conduct can provide clues that will reveal lying. This is certainly understandable, and no doubt necessary, since decisions about truthfulness—in court and in everyday life—clearly must continue to be made.

Recent studies have identified a series of behaviors that are widely assumed to be indicators of either truth or deception. Other "common sense" clues have been widely noted in the literature of trial advocacy. It is important to bear in mind that few or none of the supposed indicators have ever been shown actually to correlate with the presence or lack of veracity. In any individual witness the "suspect" conduct may as easily demonstrate nervousness as untruthfulness.

Still, trials cannot avoid judgments based upon perception, so expert witnesses must be aware that certain behavior, whatever its actual cause, is likely to be perceived as signifying either honesty or deceit.

The following sections discuss a number of the most significant aspects of demeanor, both positive and negative. This discussion is not an inventory of ploys or gimmicks. There is nothing here (or anywhere else) that will teach a witness how to trick jurors into believing them. In truth, the material that follows is more important than that—it can be used to ensure the clarity of testimony by reducing, or at least recognizing, impediments to communication.

The aim of witness preparation

INSIDE INFORMATION

Demeanor Can Make a Difference

Positive

- Posture and eye contact
- Business attire
- Concise organization
- Conversational language
- Varied format
- Illustrations and analogies

Negative

- Abrupt responses
- Rambling answers
- Hesitation
- Constant self-references
- Anger or aggression
- Arrogance or condescension
- Shifting posture or folded arms

---

1. Positive Indicators

a. Confidence and Comfort Level

It may well be that confidence is the single most powerful indicator of truthfulness. Fact finders show a clear tendency to believe witnesses who are calm, poised, and at ease when communicating directly to the judge or jury. The best way to appear confident, of course, is to be confident in the precision of your work and the validity of your opinion. Thorough preparation, accurate research, and well-organized presentation are the necessary keys to confident testimony. Having attended to the basics, an expert may then consider some of the finer points.

i. Posture and Eye Contact

In trial testimony, as in most of life, your mother had the best advice. If you want people to believe you, you have to sit up straight and look them in the eye. Posture and eye contact are important.

Even in modern courtrooms it is unlikely that the witness stands were designed with ergonomics in mind.[1] They tend to be cramped, uncomfortable, and awkwardly positioned, almost as though they were situated as an afterthought. The worst witness stands (and there are plenty of them) are set apart behind low walls with little legroom for the witness. They have hard, immovable chairs, and they often lack so much as a ledge on which the witness can place papers or exhibits. The sight lines are frequently obstructed, and poor acoustics may make it difficult to hear or be heard.

The best way to cope with a poor seating arrangement is to sit forward on the chair, plant both feet flat on the floor, and straighten your back and shoulders. Although this may not seem as relaxed as slouching, it will be more comfortable in the long run. Good posture also makes vocal projection easier. Finally, slumping or twisting in the chair creates a discomfiting impression of self-consciousness and uncertainty.

Eye contact is important, but it can also be overdone. An expert witness should not hesitate to speak directly to the fact finder, particularly during longer and more significant answers. On the other hand, a witness should avoid ostentatious or smarmy appeals to the judge or jury and should never stare at individual jurors.

ii. Good Standing

Recall that expert witnesses want to be good teachers. From kindergarten all the way through college, most teachers stand up in front of their classes. The very best teachers occupy the classroom as a virtual stage, using body movement and gestures to hold attention

---

1. In the United States it is customary for witnesses to testify while sitting down, unless they are asked to stand for the purpose of demonstrating a point or referring to an exhibit. In many other parts of the world, including the United Kingdom and other common law jurisdictions, witnesses testify while standing up.

and emphasize important points. Even the most gifted instructor would have difficulty teaching from the confines of a single chair.

Of course, witnesses cannot simply disregard the courtroom architecture. There is almost always a designated witness chair, and the witness almost always has to use it, at least at the beginning of the testimony.

Nonetheless, well-structured testimony will often afford an expert a number of opportunities to stand up. It is quite common for an expert witness to testify with the use of a projected or oversized exhibit. Rather than sitting in the chair and pointing to such an exhibit, the witness should ask permission to get up and walk over to it. The witness can then testify while standing next to the exhibit, using either her hand or a pointer to direct the fact finder's attention to important entries or characteristics. The witness should remain at the exhibit until that entire aspect of the testimony has been concluded.

To be sure, a witness should never hover over the jury or stroll aimlessly around the courtroom. Many judges have rules or procedures that govern standing or walking about the courtroom. A witness must inquire about such rules and be certain to follow them. Nonetheless, a witness should be aware that standing up gives one, well, more stature.

If you are ill at ease standing in front of an audience, you should consider practicing until you can feel comfortable while testifying upright.

iii. Attire

Most people feel and look more confident when they are comfortable in their surroundings. This inevitably raises the question of appropriate clothing. How should an expert witness dress? Which is more important, comfort or formality?

There is an obvious dress code in most courtrooms—judges wear robes and lawyers wear business attire (jackets and ties for the men and the maddeningly imprecise "equivalent" for women). Most witnesses choose to dress more or less like the lawyers.

Many physicians, social workers, scientists, academics, and engineers, among others, are now able to dress quite casually in their daily work. Accustomed to freedom from conformity and formality, they may feel uncomfortable or confined in traditional business wear. Nonetheless, unless the level of discomfort is so extraordinarily great as to impair one's ability to communicate, the best choice is usually to dress like the lawyers. You can never tell when a judge or juror might be put off by unexpected informality, but no one is ever likely to be offended by a business suit.

b. Organization

Well-organized answers are easier to follow and more likely to be understood and believed. In structure, a good answer begins with a premise or conclusion and then describes the basis for the response or the underlying facts. A concise narrative of this sort allows the fact finder to understand where the answer is headed and to follow along as the witness explains.

A kind of preview.

On the other hand, long and complex answers can be confusing, and rambling answers indicate uncertainty or indecision. Thus, narrative responses should be relatively short, generally limited to two or three sentences.

c. Conversational Language

Many studies have shown that jurors are more likely to believe witnesses whom they like or with whom they have something in common. This phenomenon, sometimes called "affinity bias," is easily recognizable from everyday life. It is easier to talk to, and therefore easier to listen to, people whose experiences seem similar to our own. In most regards there is little that an expert witness can do to affect any possible affinity links with the fact finder. Obvious characteristics—age, gender, hometown, or educational background—are all fixed long before the witness walks into the courtroom.

The expert can, however, be certain to testify while speaking the fact finder's language. Witnesses are more believable when they testify in a conversational manner. No matter what the field of expertise, there is no reason to rely on jargon or technical terms while testifying in court.

Of course, everyone expects an expert witness to have specialized knowledge, and it would surely be counterproductive to talk down to a jury. But jargon-laden, technical language will quickly take on the function of a mask or wall, dividing the expert from the fact finder and giving the impression that the witness is withholding information, or at least refraining from clarifying his testimony.

In contrast, a witness who is able to testify in conversational terms clearly indicates a willingness, perhaps even an eagerness, to make the entire testimony accessible to every member of the jury.

d. Varied Format

Varying the format of one's answers indicates that they are the product of thoughtful consideration. A witness who thinks before responding, and whose answer is geared directly to the question, is more likely to be trusted. On the other hand, answers that sound unvaried and repetitious may suggest that they are being given by rote, or even that they are rehearsed.

Consequently, expert witnesses should avoid falling into repetitive cadences. Word choice, sentence structure, length of answer, and even tone of voice should be adjusted in order to convey the precise meaning called for by the specific question. Answers should never sound as though they are being selected from a checklist.

e. Illustration

Testimony is strengthened when it can be illustrated through the use of analogies, stories, examples, and vivid descriptions. Witnesses are more credible when they draw upon these forms of expression, because they indicate an interest in communicating on a personal level.

The best analogies and examples are the original ones, initiated by the witness for the specific purpose of explaining some aspect of the case or testimony. Trite or contrived examples can detract from credibility, for the same reason that repetitive speech patterns can make testimony seem rehearsed.

2. Negative Indicators

The following sections describe a variety of verbal and nonverbal cues that are frequently assumed to be indicators of untruthfulness. In fact, none of these behaviors have ever been shown actually to demonstrate falsity, and in any given case they might all be exhibited by a scrupulously truthful witness, especially one who was nervous or under stress. Nonetheless, it will be helpful for experts to recognize the following *perceived* signs of unreliability.

a. Inappropriate Responses

Recall that conversational responses are usually the most credible answers. Consequently, an answer that is conversationally inappropriate is often taken as a sign of evasion.

One such example is the short, clipped, cut-off response. In ordinary discussions people usually speak in full sentences, or at least multiword phrases and fragments. Even if a cross-examiner's question can technically be answered "yes or no," a steady string of monosyllabic answers may appear suspiciously uncooperative, secretive, or even hostile.

At the other extreme, a chattering or run-on answer may have the identical effect by suggesting that the witness is trying use a barrage of words to camouflage an inadequate response.

b. Speech Patterns

The verbal cues most often associated with deception include hesitation, speech errors, and repeated self-references.

Hesitation must be distinguished from silence. It is often appropriate for a witness to pause briefly and spend a few moments thinking before answering. In fact, measured contemplation can be a positive indicator, especially when accompanied by an easily understood "thinking gesture" such as removing one's eyeglasses or chewing on a pencil.

Hesitation becomes a negative indicator when the silence is filled with verbal tics. Recall the expert in the previous child custody example:

QUESTION: If the situation were more drastic, wouldn't it be in this child's interest to be removed from this family?

ANSWER: Umm, well. I'd have to say, wait. Well, er, I suppose that the answer is yes.

The initial hesitation suggests a great reluctance in responding to a simple question, indicating that the witness has misgivings about the answer.

This problem can be compounded by speech errors—garbled, incomplete, or fragmentary sentences:

ANSWER: Well, drastic is more or less. I mean, you have to consider whether the child, if the parent is never, or if the situation becomes too different. So, yes, under the definite or ambiguous circumstance.

Finally, self-references can hurt. As in:

ANSWER: To be perfectly honest, that's right.

Or,

ANSWER: To tell the truth, you would have to remove a child in drastic circumstances.

Such constant refrains suggest defensiveness. Worse, they raise a question. Why does the witness have to alert us now to the fact that he is telling the truth?

c. Attitude

Anger or aggression indicate that the witness is taking the matter personally, the very opposite of a dispassionate expert. A witness will want to testify from conviction, but histrionics and overdramatization will detract from credibility. On rare occasions it may be appropriate for a witness to show resentment or indignation. For example, the witness's integrity may have been unfairly attacked, or the cross-examiner may have attempted to exploit racial or ethnic biases. Such tactics may leave the witness steaming, but even under these circumstances it is usually best to attempt to maintain composure. A calm response will often cause a scurrilous assault to backfire.

Arrogance and condescension are also attitude problems. It is true, of course, that experts are experts, called to the stand precisely because they know more about some subject than anyone else in the room. But the second qualification of an expert—teacher—is the ability to communicate the information. By definition, then, an expert should never say (or think) that the information is "too complicated" for the judge or jury.

d. Nonverbal Cues

Everyone thinks they can read body language; body language experts have even been known to testify in court. No doubt, considerable information is transmitted nonverbally, both in and out of the courtroom. But as much as people tend to rely on nonverbal cues, they are very much prone to inaccurate interpretation.

Whatever their accuracy, however, it is certain that judges and jurors will perceive certain behavior as indicative of dishonesty. The most frequently *perceived* manifestations of deceit are thought to include blinking, grinning, shifting posture, folded arms, and frequent hand movements.

F. Off the Stand

The preceding sections have all been concerned primarily with the presentation of testimony. Experts must understand, however, that they may be observed as well when they are off the stand—perhaps sitting in the courtroom, waiting in the hall, or even dining in the cafeteria. Off-the-stand behavior can also have an impact on credibility.[2]

Of course, witnesses must be careful about what they say in the hallways and elevators. Judges or jurors may be in the vicinity, and harmless comments might be half-heard or misunderstood. To the extent possible, it is best simply to avoid talking about the case in any location that is even semi-public.

It is natural, of course, for an expert to spend "break" time chatting with the retaining lawyers and perhaps the clients themselves. After all, they may be the only people in the building the expert knows. Again, however, a perfectly innocuous interchange may be misinterpreted by an observer, so it may be wisest to spend break time alone.

Finally, the expert should be aware of appearances while taking and leaving the witness stand. Though not part of the actual testimony, all eyes will certainly be focused on the expert as she walks to and from the stand. Care should be taken not to create an unpleasant or unfavorable visual impression.

Interesting

---

2.   The ethics of off-the-stand contacts are discussed in Chapter Nine, section G, *infra*.

— Chapter Three —

PREPARATION

A. Introduction

The most important aspect of any expert's work is the content and validity of her opinion. In almost every case, the great majority of the expert's time will be spent researching, considering, and preparing her opinion. Needless to say, the precise nature of that preparation will vary with the witness's field of expertise. Consequently, there can be no general approach to the "merits" of an expert's preparation to testify, other than it must be careful, independent, thorough, and reliable.

This chapter discusses the form and process of expert witness preparation, rather than its content. More specifically, it deals with the relationship between retaining counsel and the expert witness in the important areas of issue identification, information transfer, data development, and presentation. The following sections address these topics in large part through a series of questions: What should the expert contribute to the process? What should the expert expect? Request? Avoid?

Although the process of preparation is broken into four conceptual stages, it is important to recognize that the phases invariably overlap. Thus, issue identification may continue well into the period of information transfer, which may occur virtually concurrently with data development. As a general rule, however, it is fairly safe to say that issue identification comes at the beginning of the expert's work and presentation comes at the end.

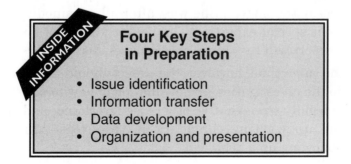

INSIDE INFORMATION

Four Key Steps in Preparation

- Issue identification
- Information transfer
- Data development
- Organization and presentation

B. Issue Identification

Once an expert has been engaged, the typical first step is issue identification. What does the lawyer need to know? The "presenting problem," so to speak, will often be stated in extremely general terms: Do the medical records indicate malpractice? What were the decedent's expected lifetime earnings? Or, depending upon the experience and sophistication of the lawyer, the initial questions may be presented in considerably more detail: Was an MRI indicated when the patient was first seen in the emergency room? What discount rate should be used in reducing damages to present value?

In any case, the lawyer's first statement of issues should be regarded only as a preliminary outline. Of course, most lawyers will understand the basic scope of a case or potential case, but the expert has considerable knowledge that the attorney lacks. Most attorneys, even very good ones, will miss issues that are easily recognizable to a skilled expert. Thus, an expert should not hesitate to consider or investigate issues beyond those first flagged by counsel.

On the other hand, there may be professionally interesting issues or questions that are, for one reason or another, not relevant to the particular lawsuit. Claims or defenses may have been settled, waived, or barred by the statute of limitations.

Consequently, the process of issue identification requires considerable give and take over the course of a litigation engagement. The expert takes initial direction from the retaining lawyer, but assumes that there is more to be learned than the lawyer necessarily realizes. At the same time, the expert recognizes her own limitations and does not presume to appreciate all of the legal aspects of the case.

For example, a medical expert might be asked to evaluate the possibility that a surgeon committed medical malpractice. In evaluating the file, perhaps the expert will come across evidence of additional errors and omissions by other physicians, nurses, or even administrators. In this situation, the expert needs to do two things. First, she must not disregard information simply because it was not mentioned by the lawyer. She was, after all, retained precisely because of her special expertise. The lawyer knows (or should know) that the expert will see things that counsel missed.

At the same time, however, the expert should not dive immediately into the investigation and evaluation of new topics. The issues might be legally irrelevant or otherwise foreclosed, and the expert could end up wasting considerable resources—time, energy, funds—following up a dead end.

The expert should understand that the legal system often re- quires questions to be approached from a particular perspective. In many jurisdictions, for instance, the legal defense of insanity de- pends on whether the defendant was capable of conforming his con- duct to the requirements of the law. Quite clearly, that is not a question that a treating psychiatrist or psychologist would usually ask, but it must be addressed if the expert's work is to be admitted at trial. In such circumstance, then, the lawyer will have to focus the professional's attention on the applicable legal rule. Other questions, no matter how essential to a full medical or psychological evaluation, need be addressed only to the extent that they have some bearing on the legal issue.

"The legal issue"

The solution lies in communication between the expert and the lawyer. Each should understand the inherent limits of his or her frame of reference, and each should be open to input from the other. At best, this should be a constant process—with the expert regularly informing the lawyer of her findings and inquiries, and the lawyer matching the expert's work to the issues in the case.

As the litigation proceeds, it will eventually be necessary to con- centrate the expert's thinking. At some point, counsel will have to de- termine which subjects are in and which are out. What, precisely, will the expert be asked to testify about on direct examination? What will be the likely scope of the anticipated cross-examination? It is the law- yer's job, not the expert's, to clarify the legal issues.

Ultimately, the expert must be provided with a definitive (or nearly definitive) statement of issues to be addressed. If the retaining lawyer fails to provide such guidance, the expert may insist upon it. It is the expert, after all, who must be fully prepared to testify, and it is the expert who may have to endure an unpleasant deposition or cross-examination. Most importantly, it is the expert whose professional integrity may be challenged, and whose reputation will suffer, if her work turns out to be incomplete, inadequate, or legally irrelevant.

C. Information Transfer

The second step in preparation is usually the transfer of informa- tion from counsel to the expert. As with issue identification, informa- tion transfer often occurs in stages. The lawyer will usually begin by giving the expert an outline of the facts of the case—perhaps orally, perhaps in the form of a letter or memorandum, perhaps by providing the pleadings or other documentation. In most cases the expert will eventually obtain from counsel a substantial body of documents, exhibits, and other data for use in arriving at her opinion.

In the relatively few cases where time and resources are unlimited, the lawyer may simply provide the witness with "everything." The expert will then have the task of sorting through stacks, folders, even boxes of material, in order to identify the salient facts. In the more usual case, information transfer will be more selective. The lawyer will first determine those items that seem most useful, and the expert will subsequently request whatever else appears necessary or helpful. Moreover, the lawyer's own access to information is not static. Whatever facts and documents the attorney possesses at the outset of the case, it is all but certain that more will be obtained through discovery as the litigation proceeds.

The next several sections discuss the various types and forms of information that may be transferred to an expert from the retaining lawyer.

1. Pleadings and Court Papers

A civil lawsuit begins when the plaintiff's attorney files a "complaint."[1] The complaint sets out the broad outline of the plaintiff's claim, identifying the defendant (or defendants) and stating why the plaintiff is entitled to relief. In most cases, the defendant will eventually be required to file an "answer" that either admits or denies each of the plaintiff's specific allegations. The answer may include "affirmative defenses," and it can also be the vehicle for raising a "counterclaim." Taken together, these documents constitute the pleadings in the case, setting out the legal issues, factual contentions, and theories of relief or defense. The pleadings are lawyers' documents, usually drafted to be simultaneously comprehensive and vague. Thus, while the pleadings define the dispute in legal terms, they are frequently of minimal assistance to the experts. Nonetheless, experts should usually review the pleadings, if for no other reason than to gain some familiarity with the identities and positions of the various parties.

As everyone knows, the process of litigation is characteristically accompanied by a tsunami of paperwork. No expert could possibly review all of the lawyers' output, nor would anyone ever want to. There will, however, be documents that may be useful to the experts' work.

---

1. Depending upon the jurisdiction and the nature of the dispute, this pleading might also be called a Petition or Application or something similar. In arbitrations, as opposed to lawsuits, the initiating document is called—unsurprisingly—a request for arbitration.

In the course of a lawsuit the issues and claims of the parties are the subject of constant revision and refinement. The lawyers will often be required to explain or justify their positions in motions, and the motions will frequently be accompanied by written arguments or briefs. What's more, the parties and witnesses themselves may file supporting affidavits[2] that fill in many additional facts. A judicious selection of motions, briefs, and affidavits may often set out a much clearer picture of the nature of the dispute, since this is one of the processes through which the attorneys initially explain the case to the judge.

Occasionally there may also be other helpful legal documents. For example, a suit may have been the subject of an earlier appeal, in which case the opinion of the appellate court may provide essential background.

2. Documents

In most cases, the retaining lawyer can be expected to provide the expert with a fair number of evidentiary documents—material that was created before the particular dispute ever arose, but which may be very important to the lawsuit. Such original documents may include letters, reports, memoranda, files, printouts, contracts, ledgers, notes, and all manner of other papers that "document" the underlying events or transactions.

The documents in a commercial case, for example, may encompass correspondence between the parties, a series of contracts and amendments, notes of meetings, bills of lading, shipping records, warehouse reports, e-mail printouts, photographs, and page after page of other papers and records. A medical malpractice case may involve hospital charts, interview notes, requisitions, test results, protocols, and various other medical records.

Preexisting documents (as opposed to those prepared for litigation) are often the best sources available to an expert, since the paperwork was probably produced at a time when the parties were not in dispute. Of course, preexisting documents are not invariably accurate. They may be informal, sloppy, ambiguous, or otherwise undependable. Nevertheless, an expert should always be on the lookout for relevant documents.

---

2. An affidavit is a written statement, signed under oath before a notary public or court officer. In some jurisdictions the requirement of notarization has been eliminated, in which case the written witness statements are called declarations.

Experts may face two somewhat related problems in reviewing documentation: too much and too little.

a. Too Much

It is hardly unknown for a lawyer to favor an expert witness with every conceivable document available in the case. While this may be manageable in a fairly simple matter, the documents in a complex civil case may number thousands or more. Worse, many of the documents may be highly technical—for example, corporate tax returns or securities filings—and therefore beyond the immediate comprehension of the witness. Apart from auditors, most experts will have little reason to examine every conceivable piece of paper in a given case.

Why do lawyers so often oversupply experts with paperwork? The cynical explanation is that lawyers tend to be lazy. It is easy to box up a ton of documents and send them to a copy service; it is painstakingly boring to go through the same documents in order to cull out the ones that might be needed by an expert. The path of least resistance is obviously to dump them all on the expert's desk and let her sort them out.[3]

A more generous answer lies somewhere between caution and good faith. A lawyer certainly never wants to fail to provide an expert with an important document—who knows whether an unproduced document might turn out to be the veritable key to the case. The surest way to avoid that risk is simply to supply everything. Even less do lawyers want to be accused of withholding documents in an effort to shape or influence the expert's opinion. Again, the remedy is to deliver it all.

Whatever the reason, an expert should not be expected to wade unaccompanied through an endless swamp of undifferentiated documents. At a minimum, the expert is entitled to a guided tour. If the lawyer cannot readily list or indicate the most relevant documents, then the expert should request a meeting where the documents can be reviewed page by page, categorized, and explained.

b. Too Little

Inundation is not the only problem when it comes to document review. Experts are often given too much, but one might also receive too little.

---

3.   It should go without saying that this is not a good sign. At the very least, a well-prepared lawyer ought to be able to identify and segregate those documents that relate to the expert's subject matter.

Of course, the absence of important papers might not be immediately obvious. Confronted with six or seven bulging notebooks, a witness might well assume that everything meaningful has been included. This is when being an expert comes in handy. Following a review of everything provided, it is useful to question the completeness of the material. Are there any gaps or obvious omissions in the records? What else should be there? What other documents might exist?

There are three potential reasons why a lawyer might fail to supply significant documents. First, the attorney may simply have erred. The papers might have been excluded inadvertently, or the lawyer might have been attempting to avoid overburdening the expert. In the same vein, counsel might not have realized the relevance of a particular set of records.

In these situations, lawyers will be happy for the expert's assistance in completing the file for review. Experts should always feel free to ask for more documents, especially when they are of the sort that "ought" to exist, given the nature of the documentation and the context of the case.

This brings us to the second possibility—the lawyer may not have all of the documents. The client, for whatever reason, may have neglected to give everything to counsel. Of more concern is the possibility that opposing counsel has failed to comply fully with discovery requests. For example, assume that an expert has been retained to arrive at an opinion concerning a patient's psychiatric care. In reviewing the medical records the expert realized that there were no clinical interview notes. A lawyer, untrained in the ways of hospitals and psychiatric treatment, would not necessarily notice the missing documents. Thus, it falls to the expert to bring the problem to the attention of counsel, who should be extremely pleased to learn of the apparent gap in the documentation. Thanks to the expert's perceptiveness, the notes can now be sought or requested.

Finally, we must entertain the bleak possibility that counsel has intentionally withheld documents in an effort to color the expert's opinion. This does not happen often, if only because the risk to counsel of withholding information is usually greater than the reward. Still, an expert should never be placed in the position of having her opinion "massaged" through the selective presentation of information. If that appears to be happening, the expert should either correct the situation immediately or resign the engagement.

3. Depositions and Discovery Responses

a. Depositions

A deposition is an oral statement, given under oath, as part of the pretrial discovery process. Lawyers take depositions in order to learn what the witnesses have to say, and therefore the scope of testimony is not nearly so limited as it would be at trial. Deposition transcripts are often hundreds of pages long, covering everything that might conceivably be relevant to the particular case.

Obviously, then, deposition transcripts can be extraordinarily good sources of information for experts. Depositions often provide the best possible window on "what happened," or at least on what the various witnesses have claimed about what happened.

Experts should generally attempt to review all of the deposition testimony that might be germane to the expert's opinion. Of course, this does not mean that every expert must read every word of every deposition. There will often be volumes of testimony that have no bearing at all on the expert's subject matter. Some transcripts may have a only a few pertinent pages, though the deposition itself went on for several days.

One caution is called for when it comes to reading depositions. The purpose of a deposition is merely to discover what the witness knows. Except in rare cases, the deposition is not intended to be a substitute for trial testimony. Consequently, the examinations are frequently disorganized, disjointed, and discontinuous. The lawyers jump from subject to subject, raising and dropping points, returning to earlier topics, and generally making no attempt to elicit a single, linear narrative. Thus, information useful to a particular expert might well be scattered throughout the transcript—a page here, a paragraph there. One should make few assumptions about the completeness or coherence of a line of deposition testimony.

As with documents, it is easily possible for an expert to be burdened by too many deposition transcripts. It is also possible to omit an important deposition or to skip significant testimony while reading the transcripts one has received. It is particularly important, therefore, to work closely with counsel in determining which depositions, and which parts of depositions, the expert will review.

Finally, be aware that experts may be retained at virtually any stage of the litigation. It is common, though regrettable, for an attorney to begin approaching experts only after discovery has been completed and all of the depositions have been taken. In these circumstances, the expert can only read the testimony that has already been produced. It is not unusual for the expert to read through a transcript, wondering all the while why the most important question was never asked. This happens, of course, because the deposing lawyer was shooting in the dark—entirely unaware of the facts and queries that would eventually be meaningful to an expert witness.

Lawyers who are better organized or more deliberate, however, will tend to engage experts early in the litigation process, prior to taking any depositions. The experts in those cases are fortunate indeed, since they can participate in deposition planning and request that certain questions be asked or lines of inquiry be pursued.

To take a simple example from the previous chapter, imagine that a financial expert has been retained to evaluate cost overruns on a construction project. The litigation has been in progress for several years, and all of the nonexpert depositions have been taken. After reviewing the available records, the expert has a question for the retaining attorney:

EXPERT: How were the labor allocations coded on this job?

LAWYER: Huh? What does that mean?

EXPERT: How did they decide which workers' hours would be charged to which tasks on the job site?

LAWYER: Why do you need to know that?

EXPERT: It is important to a determination of the overrun, since it will help me distinguish between necessary and unnecessary expenses.

LAWYER: Well, how would I find out the answer?

EXPERT: It shouldn't be too hard. Just ask the project superintendent. Don't you get to take a deposition?

LAWYER: Oops.

Now, imagine instead that the expert was retained early in the case, before any of the important depositions were taken:

LAWYER: I am taking the deposition of the project superintendent next week. Is there anything you need to know?

EXPERT: I would really like to find out how the labor allocations were coded on the job.

LAWYER: No problem, but what does that mean?

> EXPERT: Ask them how they decided which workers' hours would be charged to which tasks on the job site.
>
> LAWYER: Sounds important. I can probably get more useful information if you explain a little more about why you need it.
>
> Prepared in this manner, the deposition will obviously be more useful to both expert and attorney.

b. Discovery Responses

In addition to depositions, parties are also usually required to file written responses to discovery.

i. Interrogatories

Interrogatories—written questions to be answered under oath—are the most common form of written discovery.

Interrogatory answers may frequently be of little help to experts, however, since the responses are drafted by opposing counsel and seldom contain useful narratives. From an expert's perspective, the best interrogatories are usually those that seek objective information in the form of statistics or data compilations. Consider two possible interrogatories in an unfair trade practices case. First, an interrogatory that seeks a narrative answer:

> INTERROGATORY: Describe in detail the plaintiff company's plans for expansion.

The lawyer-drafted answer might well read something like this:

> ANSWER: The plaintiff company intends to expand in a well-planned, strategically effective manner, taking advantage of all good market opportunities but avoiding overextension.

Though a financial expert would want to be aware of that answer, it surely is unlikely to figure prominently in arriving at the expert's opinion. Now consider an interrogatory that seeks data compilation:

> INTERROGATORY: List every location examined or inspected by agents of defendant company as a possible site for future expansion.

This interrogatory will produce a list of potential expansion sites, thus providing the expert with at least some hard information.

As with depositions, then, interrogatories are more likely to be useful when counsel obtains the expert's input in the drafting process. Working alone, an attorney can only guess at what data an expert might need to arrive at a meaningful opinion. The expert, of course, knows for sure.

ii. Disclosure Statements

The parties to litigation in federal courts are formally required to provide each other with written disclosure statements containing (1) the names and addresses of all witnesses, and the subject matter on which they have information; (2) a list identifying all relevant documents; and (3) a computation of any category of claimed damages.

These disclosure statements are likely to be of limited use to experts, but they should certainly be examined. Note that a number of local federal courts have chosen to opt out of the mandatory disclosure provisions of the Federal Rules.

iii. Expert Reports

Under the Federal Rules of Civil Procedure, expert witnesses are required to prepare reports, which must then be provided to the opposing parties. Under the Rules,

> The report shall contain a complete statement of all opinions to be expressed and basis and reasons therefor; the data or other information considered by the witness in forming the opinions; the qualifications of the witness, including a list of all publications authored by the witness within the preceding ten years; the compensation to be paid for the study and testimony; and a listing of any other cases in which the witness has testified as an expert at trial or by deposition within the preceding four years.[4]

Expert reports tend not to be required in state courts, though there may be other forms of obligatory disclosure. Additionally, retaining counsel may sometimes request that an expert prepare a report whether or not mandated by a statute or rule.

It should go without saying that one will always want to review the reports of opposing experts.[5] Note, however, that even in federal

---

4. Rule 26(a)(2), Federal Rules of Civil Procedure.
5. The preparation of an expert's own report will be discussed in section E.2, *infra*.

cases the requirement of expert reports may be waived by the court or the parties.

```
INSIDE INFORMATION

Mandatory Disclosures
Under Federal Rules

• Statement of all opinions
• Bases for all opinions
• Data or information considered
• Exhibits
• Qualifications
• Publications (preceding ten years)
• Compensation
• Prior testimony (preceding four years)
```

4. Assumptions

Another method of transferring information is through the use of assumptions and stipulations.

There will often be facts in litigation that a lawyer expects to be able to prove at trial, but that cannot be definitively located in a specific document, pleading, or deposition. Or, in the case of an early retention, there may be facts that are fairly certain to be established, but that have not yet been nailed down in documentary form. In these and similar circumstances, it is reasonable for the retaining lawyer to ask an expert to "assume" certain things about the case.

Depending upon the nature of the case, it is appropriate for an expert to base some or all of her opinion upon assumptions provided by the retaining lawyer. Though not absolutely necessary, it is always best for such assumptions to be reduced to writing, perhaps in the form of a letter or memorandum. Alternatively, the expert might be asked to assume the accuracy of certain facts as set out in a pleading, motion, or brief.

In every case, of course, some facts are in dispute. The plaintiff says one thing, and the defendant claims the exact opposite. No expert can be expected to resolve such competing claims; that is a job for the judge or jury. If the contested facts are necessary to the expert's opinion, assumptions can be used in two different ways. First, the expert could be asked simply to assume the facts favorable to the retaining party. Of course, the expert's opinion in this event could be no better than the validity of the assumption. If the facts are eventually proven otherwise, the expert's opinion will be undermined.

Another approach is for the expert to make alternative assumptions. First, evaluate the problem under the plaintiff's facts, and then reevaluate the case using the defendant's version of events. In an automobile accident case, for example, assume that the defendant claimed he was driving at 30 miles per hour, but the plaintiff testified he was going at least 15 miles faster. Rather than attempt to resolve this disagreement, an expert witness could undertake two analyses of stopping distance, once assuming a 30 mile per hour rate of speed, and again assuming 45 miles per hour.

Whatever the source or manner of the assumptions, it is the expert's job to be certain they are reasonable under the circumstances. In the above scenario, for example, the expert should not be willing to assume that an automobile was traveling 180 miles per hour—unless the accident took place on a racetrack.

5. Stipulations and Judicial Admissions

A stipulation is an agreement between the parties that certain facts are true. Once facts have been stipulated, they are regarded as proven for all purposes in the litigation.[6] Experts may therefore always rely on stipulations when reaching their opinions.

A judicial admission is a binding statement made by a party (or a party's lawyer) in the course of a lawsuit. Judicial admissions are most often made in reply to pleadings or in response to a special discovery device called, not surprisingly, "requests for admission."[7] Whatever the form, a judicial admission conclusively establishes the admitted fact, though only for the purpose of case in which it is made. Experts are obviously entitled to rely upon judicial admissions.

6. Details

As we have seen, information may be transferred from counsel to expert through a variety of means. Whatever the format of the transfer, there are certain types of information that an expert will usually want to be certain to receive from retaining counsel.

Chronology. Because time is linear, every case has a chronology. Though it may be more important in some matters than in others, a sequence of events is almost always useful to an expert witness. Of course, the chronology of a case may often be extracted from the pleadings and documents, but that can be a time-consuming and

---

6. It is conceivable, though unusual, that facts might be stipulated for a limited purpose. Counsel will no doubt inform the experts when that is the case.

7. Rule 36, Federal Rules of Civil Procedure.

erratic process, especially in a complex, multiwitness case. At some point, therefore, it will be helpful for the expert and lawyer to sit down together to draw a time line, placing the significant events in strict, chronological order.

Cast of characters. As with the chronology, the names and positions of important witnesses may be gleaned from source materials. The process may be made quicker and more reliable, however, if counsel simply provides the witness with a list of dramatis personae.

History. The prior dealings or past involvement of the parties (or witnesses) may be useful to an expert witness. Background never hurts.

Prior statements. An expert should be provided with all of the prior statements of every witness whose testimony may be germane to the expert's opinion.

Opposing experts. Have experts been identified by the other side? If so, who are they and what have they had to say? What data and information did they use? What assumptions did they make? What methods did they use?

Opposing counsel. Who is the opposing counsel, and is there anything notable about him or her that the expert ought to know?

Contrary facts. What is the opposing party's position in the case? What is the factual basis for the opposing party's claim? What facts might undermine or detract from the expert's opinion? What contrary assumptions might the expert be asked about at deposition or on cross-examination?

INSIDE INFORMATION

Information Transfer Checklist

☐ Pleadings and court papers
☐ Documents
☐ Depositions
☐ Discovery responses
☐ Assumptions
☐ Stipulations
☐ Judicial admissions
☐ Details

D. Data Development

At some point in most engagements, an expert will need to develop data beyond that which was supplied by the retaining attorney. The precise type of data, of course, will depend upon the individual's field of expertise. In that regard, expert witnesses can be divided generally into three broad categories:[8]

Categories of Experts

Experts who calculate

Experts who test, measure, or record

Experts who evaluate or critique

- Experts who calculate, including accountants, appraisers, economists, actuaries, demographers, and statisticians.

- Experts who test, measure, or record, including engineers, chemists, physicists, toxicologists, psychologists, photographers, and fingerprint examiners.

- Experts who evaluate or critique, including physicians, lawyers, dentists, and "human factors" or safety experts.

There is no way, of course, to classify or pigeonhole the exact type of work an expert will need to do in any particular case. A "calculation" expert may need to obtain government or industry statistics, or she may have to design and conduct her own independent survey. A "testing" expert may need to perform a series of scientific comparisons. An "evaluating" expert may need to do a literature search or other research.

---

8. These categories were developed by Deanne C. Siemer in "Demonstrative Evidence and Expert Witnesses," in Faust F. Rossi, *Expert Witnesses* (1991).

Depending upon the nature of the litigation, independent data development may comprise the bulk of the expert's work—as in the case of a demographer or examining psychologist. In other situations it may be a relatively modest undertaking—as with a "human factors" expert whose work is primarily an evaluation of past events. The extent of data development is often within the expert's professional discretion. For example, a pathologist in a medical malpractice case may believe it sufficient to examine existing records, but in extreme circumstances it might actually be necessary to request an exhumation and new autopsy.

Whatever the field of expertise, the witness should make sure that retaining counsel understands the need and extent of the necessary independent data development.

One final caution. An expert's work in data compilation is generally discoverable by the opposing party. Thus, all notes, work papers, drafts, protocols, models, memoranda, and other preliminary work may well be turned over to the other side. Knowing this, a competent expert will take care that her notes are not misleading or subject to misinterpretation or distortion (intentional or otherwise) by opposing counsel.

E. Organization and Presentation

The final stage of preparation is usually the organization and presentation of the expert's opinion. In this context, "presentation" refers to the formal pretrial statement of the expert's opinion, and not to testimony at deposition or trial.

1. Format

The first step in presenting an opinion is determining the format required by the case. As noted above, the rules in federal court now require experts to submit reports prior to testifying. The corresponding rules vary in state jurisdictions. In some states the expert must prepare a report, in others she must provide written answers to certain questions, and in a number of states the expert need only show up ready to testify at trial.

Even in states where no formal report is required, retaining counsel may sometimes prefer to have the expert write one. A written report can be useful in a number of ways. A comprehensive, well-reasoned, authoritative opinion may be persuasive in settlement discussions with opposing counsel. It can aid the attorney in organizing his own thinking about the case, and it can be helpful in ensuring that lawyer and witness are "on the same page."[9]

If possible, the expert should determine at the outset of an engagement whether a report will ultimately be required or requested. Research and preparation, not to mention note taking, may be different when the expert's work must eventually result in a written product.

2. Writing a Report

a. Content

Under the federal rules, an expert's report must include the following:

- A complete statement of all opinions to be expressed by the expert.
- The basis and reasons for the expert's opinions.
- The data or information considered by the witness in forming the opinions.
- Any exhibits to be used as a summary of or support for the opinions.
- The qualifications of the witness, including a list of all publications in the preceding ten years.
- The compensation to be paid for the study and testimony.
- A list of any other cases in which the witness has testified as an expert (at trial or in deposition) within the preceding four years.

This format provides a useful template that can be employed whenever a report is to be written. The last two items—compensation and prior testimony—may often be omitted from reports in state jurisdictions, though the information is almost certainly discoverable in one manner or another.

b. Organization

The federal rules do not mandate a particular format for an expert's report, leaving the witness free to organize the material as effectively as possible. While the minimal purpose of disclosure is simply to inform the other side of the content of (and support for) the

---

9. In jurisdictions where reports are optional, the retaining lawyer will have to weigh the benefits of having a written document against the drawbacks—including the need to produce any report to the opposing parties. This is a decision for the lawyer to make; an expert should not draft a report without prior consultation with counsel.

expert's opinion, it will often be preferable, and probably easier, to write a more "narrative" report.

A narrative report will, in essence, tell the story of the expert's opinion, attempting to make it as readily understandable as possible. An expert's report is not a technical document directed to other professionals in the expert's field. Rather, it is intended to be read and comprehended by the lawyers in the case, and perhaps by a judge and jury as well. Thus, the explanatory overview is often the most important part of the report.

Most reports begin with an introductory segment, including a summary of the expert's qualifications. Then, rather than attempting to subdivide the opinion into discrete components or fragments, the report will set out a clear, comprehensive statement of the expert's ultimate conclusions. The report will next explain the theory or summary that underlies the opinion, and will then explain the analysis or thought processes the expert used to reach her conclusions. Finally, the report will list supporting data or documents.

Thus, the broad outline of an expert's report might be as follows:

Introduction. A brief statement of the expert's involvement in the case, including a summary of her most salient qualifications.

Statement of opinion. A concise statement of the expert's ultimate conclusion or conclusions in the case. For example, a financial expert in a cost overrun case might state, "It is my opinion that the changes requested by the general contractor resulted in significant additional work by the electrical subcontractor that was not covered by the original contract. I have calculated the cost of that work as $340,000."

Overview. Here the expert will explain, as simply as possible, the theory or process that underlies her opinion. For example, "I reached my opinion by examining all of the subcontractor's direct and indirect costs on this project, including labor, materials, and overhead. Relying upon the job site records and the report of a consulting engineer, I determined which costs were attributable to the original contract and which were attributable to 'change orders.' I then calculated the proportion of labor and materials devoted to the change orders and I used that ratio to allocate overhead."

Analysis. This will probably be the longest segment of the report, explaining why the expert chose a certain approach and detailing the step-by-step process of analysis or application. Depending upon the nature of the case, this section may include tables, summary charts, or other exhibits.

Supporting data. Supporting data, though important to the expert's opinion, may be difficult for a lay reader to understand or appreciate. It is therefore usually best to leave it to the end of the report, probably listed in a separate section.

Note that many of the necessary components of a report may be submitted as attachments or appendices. For example, the expert's curriculum vitae may be attached in fulfillment of the "qualifications and publications" requirement. Similarly, documents and other data reviewed may be listed in an appendix, as can be prior testimony.

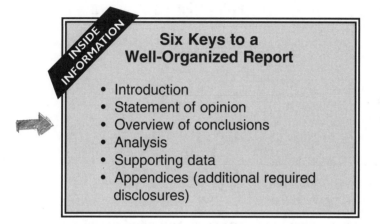

INSIDE INFORMATION

Six Keys to a Well-Organized Report

- Introduction
- Statement of opinion
- Overview of conclusions
- Analysis
- Supporting data
- Appendices (additional required disclosures)

Before drafting a report, it is prudent for the expert to discuss its precise scope with retaining counsel. As noted above in the issue identification section,[10] the expert will want to be certain to deal with all of the legally significant issues and to discuss them in the context of the pertinent legal standards. In addition, the retaining lawyer might want to instruct the expert to address or omit certain issues. For example, one might be extremely critical of the work or ideas of an expert for the opposing party. Nonetheless, counsel may legitimately choose not to make such criticism a part of the case. Thus, it is up to the lawyer to decide whether or not the critique of the opposition theory should be included in the expert's report.[11]

In writing reports, experts should be aware that their notes and preliminary drafts may be subject to discovery.

---

10. See section B, *supra*.

11. It should go without saying that the lawyer may only determine *which* issues will be addressed by an expert. The lawyer certainly may not tell the expert what to say about those issues.

3. Visual Aids

An expert witness, together with retaining counsel, should always consider the use of visual aids to enhance the presentation of the expert's opinion.

— Chapter Four —

DIRECT EXAMINATION

A. Introduction

For an expert witness, direct examination may be understood as the intersection of credibility and preparation. Thus, the two preceding chapters combine to bring us right up to the trial itself. The expert has done her work diligently and thoroughly. The research is finished, the documents have been reviewed and assimilated, the literature has been studied, the report has been written. As far as she knows, there are no unturned stones.

The expert realizes that her credibility may well depend upon her ability to organize and communicate the material. She has considered her role as a teacher, and she has thought through the overview that will best make her conclusions accessible to the fact finder.[1]

In short, she is ready for direct examination.

B. The Role of Direct Examination

For counsel, direct examination is the heart of the case. It is the fulcrum of the trial—the aspect upon which all else turns. It is the advocate's opportunity to present the facts necessary to prevail.

While lay people usually look forward to cross-examination as the most challenging part of the trial, the truth is that direct examination is generally more important and frequently more complex and demanding. From the lawyer's perspective, a good cross-examination can focus on one or two small points, honing in on a few weaknesses or inconsistencies. A good direct examination, however, must tell the entire story—and must tell it logically and dynamically. This is no mean feat. Typically an effective direct examination must sort through and organize a great mass of information, paring it down to the essential elements, and presenting it in an interesting and

---

1. See Chapter Two, section B, *supra*.

understandable manner. For experts in particular, this can be difficult indeed.

In a good direct examination, the witness is the center of attention. While the lawyer devises and asks the questions, it is the witness who must carry forward the weight of the narrative. The questions, by law, must be non-leading. This means that they will be short and open: What did you do? Why did you do it? What is your opinion? How did you reach it?

In a sense, the lawyer sets the stage, makes the introductions, and supplies the transitions. The witness teaches the class, providing the overview, explaining the theory, and filling in the supportive details. For an expert witness, the goal of direct examination is to educate the fact finder. To be effective, the expert must provide her opinion, explain its foundation, substantiate its basis, present her data—and do this all while focusing the fact finder's attention on material that may be complicated, unfamiliar, and—let's face it—intrinsically boring.

The key to direct examination, therefore, is the expert's theory. No direct examination will succeed (and no cross-examination will be necessary) if the witness simply drones through a welter of facts, details, technicalities, or statistics. To understand an expert's testimony, the fact finder must first be given a window into its meaning. That window, as we have discussed before and will discuss again, is the expert's theory.

C. Offering Expert Testimony

There is a certain logic to the direct examination of most experts. While the particulars will vary, there are, in fact, a limited number of possible patterns for organizing an expert's testimony. It is absolutely necessary, for example, to qualify the expert before proceeding to her opinion. The following sections present, in broad outline, a common format for expert testimony.

1. Introduction and Foreshadowing

The first step in direct examination is usually to introduce the expert and explain her involvement in the case. Since expert testimony is qualitatively different from lay testimony, counsel will often want to clarify its purposes for the jury members so that they will understand what they are about to hear.[2] Thus, the witness will

---

2. In a bench trial, it is unlikely that a lawyer will take the time to explain the purpose of expert testimony. If the judge does not already understand it, explaining will not help.

probably be asked how she came to be retained and why she is present in court.

> Moreover, the technical requirements of presenting expert testimony often result in a considerable time lag between the introduction of the witness and the substantive high points of her testimony. Lawyers solve this problem by "foreshadowing" the expert's opinion at the very outset of the examination.

In the following example, the plaintiff operated a statewide chain of drive-in restaurants but was put out of business by the defendant's allegedly unfair, predatory (and therefore illegal) competitive practices. The plaintiff's financial expert is now being introduced to the jury:

E.g.

QUESTION: Please state your name.

ANSWER: Dr. Sarah Lipton.

QUESTION: Dr. Lipton, have you been retained to reach an expert opinion in this case?

ANSWER: Yes, I was asked to evaluate the plaintiff's lost profits.

QUESTION: Did you reach an opinion concerning the amount of the plaintiff's lost profits?

ANSWER: Yes, I have calculated the amount of money that the plaintiff would have earned if the restaurants had been able to continue in business.

QUESTION: We'll get into the details of your opinion in a few minutes, but right now we have to talk about your qualifications to testify as an expert in this case.

2. Qualification

To testify as an expert, a witness must be qualified by reason of knowledge, skill, experience, training, or education.[3] This is a "threshold" question for the judge, who must determine whether the witness is appropriately qualified before permitting her to give opinion testimony.

For the expert, the qualification segment is often awkward. It can be uncomfortable, sitting before a roomful of strangers, to catalog one's awards, accomplishments, and achievements. An extended

3. Rule 702, Federal Rules of Evidence. For a discussion of the technical requirements of qualification, see Chapter One, section C, *supra*.

rendition of schools attended and articles written can also be boring and tiresome, making it difficult to maintain the attention of the fact finder. Nonetheless, qualification of the witness is a necessary predicate for all of the testimony to follow.

a. Technical Requirements

The technical requirements for qualifying an expert are straightforward. It is usually adequate to show that the witness possesses some specialized skill or knowledge, acquired through appropriate experience or education, and that the witness is able to apply that skill or knowledge in a manner relevant to the issues in the case.

The minimal qualifications for the plaintiff's damages expert in the restaurant case could be established as follows:

QUESTION: Dr. Lipton, could you please tell us something about your education?

ANSWER: Certainly. I have an undergraduate degree in mathematics from Northwestern University and a Ph.D. in economics from the University of California.

QUESTION: What work have you done since receiving your doctorate?

ANSWER: I was a professor in the economics department at the University of Pennsylvania for six years. Then I left to start my own consulting firm, which is called Lipton & Associates.

QUESTION: Do you have a specialty within the field of economics?

ANSWER: Yes, my specialty is business valuation.

QUESTION: Has business valuation been your specialty both at the University of Pennsylvania and at Lipton & Associates?

ANSWER: Yes.

QUESTION: Could you explain the field of business valuation?

ANSWER: It is the study of all of the components that contribute to the fair value of a business, including anticipated future profits, assets, receivables, goodwill, and investment potential.

The above example confirms the expert's qualifications by reason of both education and experience. Dr. Lipton should now be able to give an opinion as to the projected profits for the restaurant chain.

There are, of course, many other areas of basic qualifications beyond education and business experience. Possibilities include specialized training, continuing education courses, part-time teaching and lecturing positions, licenses and certifications, publications, consulting experience, professional memberships, awards, and other professional honors.

b. Additional Qualification

Concerning any given field, the retaining attorney may not be aware of the significance of particular experience, certifications or achievements—and not all of the most important points will necessarily be listed on the expert's curriculum vitae. Consequently, it can be extremely useful for the expert to share with counsel a list of what she believes to be her most salient qualifications to present an opinion in the case at trial. This may be especially appreciated in cases involving so-called "dueling experts," since counsel may well need some additional insight into the significance of various qualifications.

It is a mistake, however, to think that more qualifications are necessarily more impressive. An endless repetition of degrees, publications, awards, and appointments may easily overload any judge or juror's ability, not to mention desire, to pay careful attention to the witness. For that reason, lawyers often choose to offer as evidence the expert's detailed resume or curriculum vitae, and to use the qualification portion of the actual examination to focus on a few of the most meaningful points.

An expert's credibility may be greatly enhanced by singling out qualifications that relate specifically to the particular case. Thus, it would be important to point out that the witness has written several articles directly relevant to the issues in the case. It would be less useful to go through a long list of extraneous publications, even if they appeared in prestigious professional journals. Other case-specific qualifications may include direct experience, consulting work, or teaching that is connected to an issue in the lawsuit.

Experience is often more significant than academic background. So, for example, a medical expert may be more impressive if she has actually practiced in the applicable specialty, as opposed to possessing knowledge that is strictly theoretical—unless, of course, theoretical matters go to the heart of the case.

c. Tender of the Witness

In some jurisdictions it is necessary, once qualifications have be concluded, for the attorney to "tender" the witness to the court as an expert in a specified field. The purpose of the tender is to inform the court that qualification has been completed and to give opposing counsel an opportunity either to conduct a "voir dire" examination [4] of the witness or to object to the claim of expertise. In the restaurant example above, the financial expert would be tendered as follows:

COUNSEL: Your Honor, we tender Dr. Sarah Lipton as an expert witness in the fields of economics, business valuation, and the projection of profits.

The tender of a witness is often perfunctory, drawing no objection, and resulting in the court's pronouncement that the witness may indeed testify as an expert. On occasion, however, the tender may be the flash point for an intense struggle over the witness's qualifications—either through argument or by way of continued examination by every attorney in the case.

3. Opinion and Theory

Following qualification, the next step in the direct examination of an expert witness is often to elicit definitive statements of opinion and theory.

a. Statement of Opinion

The rules in federal court provide that an expert "may testify in terms of opinion or inference and give his reasons therefor without prior disclosure of the underlying facts or data, unless the court requires otherwise."[5] Consequently, once the witness has been qualified (and accepted as an expert in jurisdictions requiring a formal tender and ruling), she may be asked immediately to express her opinion without additional foundation or background. In other words, she may state her conclusions without first being asked to detail the nature or extent of her underlying work or investigation.

This "opinion first" approach may seem unnatural to the witness. In day-to-day life, and in most professional situations, we usually give our reasons before we state our conclusions, not after. Many attorneys, however, believe quite strongly in taking advantage of the "opinion first"

---

4. Voir dire is a limited cross-examination that temporarily suspends the direct so that the opposing attorney may inquire into the expert's qualifications.

5. Rule 705, Federal Rules of Evidence.

option. Expert testimony can tend to be long, arcane, and tedious. The intricate details of the expert's preparation are unlikely to be interesting or even particularly understandable. They will be even less captivating if they are offered in a void, without any advance notice of where the details are leading or why they are being explained.

A clear statement of the expert's conclusion can provide the context for the balance of the explanatory testimony. Compare the following vignettes, each taken from the drive-in restaurant example earlier.

QUESTION: Dr. Lipton, what did you do to arrive at your opinion in this matter?

ANSWER: My first step was to gather all of the available data regarding vehicle registrations and anticipated population growth in the state.

QUESTION: Then what did you do?

ANSWER: I correlated population growth with expected vehicle miles to arrive at a reasonable estimate of "miles per person" over each of the next five years.

QUESTION: How was that calculation performed?

Even the most diligent and attentive juror would be baffled by this examination; even the expert's mother would have difficulty paying attention. What is the relevance of vehicle miles to fast-food profits? What does population growth have to do with predatory competitive practices? The nature of the witness's computation is meaningless in the absence of some connection to her opinion in the case. Indeed, the more thoroughly the witness explains her calculations, the more incomprehensible they will become to a lay fact finder.

In contrast, consider the following:

QUESTION: Dr. Lipton, do you have an opinion as to the profits that the plaintiff's restaurant chain would have made, if it hadn't been forced out of business?

ANSWER: Yes, I do.

QUESTION: What is your opinion?

ANSWER: According to my calculations, the restaurant chain would have earned at least $3.2 million over the next five years, if it had been able to stay in business.

QUESTION: How did you reach that opinion?

ANSWER: I based my calculations on the state's projected population growth, combined with the probable demand for fast-food, drive-in restaurants.

The second examination is far more understandable. By providing her opinion at the outset the expert allows the trier of fact to comprehend the significance of the details that follow. The jury will now be much more able to understand the relationship between lost profits and the data on vehicle registration and population growth.

---

b. Statement of Theory

As we have discussed throughout this book, an expert's opinion is only as good as the theory that explains it. Consequently, once the expert's opinion has been stated, the direct examiner will often ask the witness to proceed immediately to the underlying theory.

An expert witness's theory should furnish the nexus between the expert's conclusion and the data used to support the conclusion. In other words, the direct examination will ask the witness to follow this pattern: (1) What is your opinion? (2) What are the principles that support your opinion? (3) What did you do in reaching your final conclusions?

In the drive-in restaurant example, the expert's theory should explain *why* population growth and vehicle miles are reliable indicators of projected profits:

QUESTION: Dr. Lipton, why did you base your calculations on the state's projected population growth?

ANSWER: The demand for fast-food will rise as population grows. This is particularly true because teenagers and parents of young children are the largest purchasers of fast-food, and they are also two of the groups that increase most rapidly as population goes up.

QUESTION: Why did you also consider growth in vehicle miles?

ANSWER: Drive-in restaurants are especially sensitive to vehicle miles. As people drive more, they are exposed to more drive-in restaurants, and they therefore buy more meals.

QUESTION: What did you conclude from these relationships?

ANSWER: I concluded that the profitability of a drive-in restaurant chain will rise in proportion to a combination of general population growth and increases in miles driven.

QUESTION: Did you consider only population growth and vehicle miles?

ANSWER: Of course not. I began by determining the chain's profits under current conditions, and I used those figures as a base. Then I projected them forward for five years, using the government's statistics for population and driving.

QUESTION: Please tell us how you did that.

Business valuation is not a simple subject. There is probably nothing that will make it gripping or inspiring, and few if any jurors will be able to grasp fully the witness's use of statistics and projections. But note how the theory-driven examination provides the context for the detailed explanation that will follow.

4. Explanation and Support

Having stated her opinion and supported it with a theory, the expert can now go on to detail the nature of her investigation and calculations. The fact finder cannot be expected to take the expert at her word, so the validity and accuracy of her data and assumptions should be established.

a. Data

The expert will probably be asked how she chose and obtained her data, and why her information is reliable. A scientific expert, no doubt, will be asked about the validity and results of any tests, experiments, or comparisons.

In the scenario above, for example, the expert would be expected to point out that government statistics on population and vehicle miles are used to make many crucial decisions, such as the configuration of traffic lights, the expansion of highways, and even construction of schools.

The treatment of underlying data is often one of the touchiest aspects of expert testimony. Many experts will be in love with their data, and they will be anxious to lay them out in excruciating detail. Unfortunately, most judges and jurors will have little tolerance for lengthy descriptions of enigmatic scientific or technical processes.

The challenge, therefore, is to strike a balance, providing a sufficiently detailed treatment of the data to establish its reliability but stopping well short of the point where the fact finder's attention span is exhausted.

Finally, note that it is not sufficient for the expert simply to relate the nature of the data. Rather, the witness should go on to explain how and why the data support her conclusions.

b. Assumptions

Most experts rely upon assumptions of one sort or another. The financial expert in the fast-food case, for example, would no doubt assume that the relationship between sales and population growth would continue at historical rates. The expert would also probably assume a certain financial "discount rate" for reducing the dollars in her projection to present value. There is obviously nothing wrong with using appropriate assumptions, but their validity should be explained:

QUESTION: Dr. Lipton, did you make any assumptions in reaching your opinion that the plaintiff's restaurant chain would have earned $3.2 million in profits?

ANSWER: Yes, I assumed that fast-food sales would continue to increase in proportion to population at the same rate as they had in the past.

QUESTION: Why did you make that assumption?

ANSWER: The restaurant chain had been put out of business, so there were no actual sales to look at. I therefore had to project their most likely sales, and for that I had to assume a base figure to project forward.

QUESTION: What did you use as your base figure?

ANSWER: I used the average growth for the entire industry.

QUESTION: Why did you use the industry average?

ANSWER: I used the industry average precisely because it is an average of all of the companies in that particular business. That way I could be sure that I wasn't using a figure that was abnormally high or abnormally low.

It is not necessary, and probably not possible, to explain or outline every single hypothesis used in reaching an opinion. The more important assumptions, however, should be noted, explained, and supported.

5. Theory Differentiation

In cases involving so-called "dueling experts," there will almost certainly also be competing theories. Each expert will be asked to explain why her theory is the right one.

Taking the disagreement one step further, it is not unusual for a witness to be asked to comment on the opposing expert's work. This segment of the examination is sometimes called "theory differentiation," since the witness is asked to address the shortcomings or failings of the other expert's theory.

In the previous sections we have seen illustrations taken from the testimony of the plaintiff's financial expert in a case involving a restaurant chain's lost profits. Now consider this example of theory differentiation, offered by the expert witness for the defendant:[6]

QUESTION: Please state your name.

ANSWER: Nathan Isaacs.

QUESTION: Dr. Isaacs, have you had an opportunity to review the work done in this case by Dr. Sarah Lipton?

ANSWER: Yes, I have examined Dr. Lipton's report and work papers.

QUESTION: Do you agree with Dr. Lipton's damage projections?

ANSWER: No, I do not.

QUESTION: Why not?

ANSWER: Dr. Lipton based her estimate on a combination of population growth and mileage assumptions, and this approach cannot yield a reliable result.

QUESTION: Why is that?

ANSWER: Because it assumes too much. Dr. Lipton's theory is that restaurant revenues will naturally rise

---

6. For the purpose of this example, assume that the witness has already been identified and qualified.

along with population and automobile miles. While this might possibly be true for the entire restaurant industry, there is no reason to think that it would be true for any particular drive-in chain. To reach a dependable result for an individual chain you would have to consider many other factors.

QUESTION: What factors are those?

ANSWER: At a minimum you would have to consider location, market niche, product recognition, potential competition, specific demographics, and general economic climate.

QUESTION: Did Dr. Lipton consider those factors?

ANSWER: There is no mention of them in either her report or her work papers.

QUESTION: Could you please give us an example of how location could affect the profit projections?

ANSWER: Certainly. Population always grows unevenly. Even if the overall population rises in a state or a city, it might stay constant or fall in certain areas. Therefore, a restaurant chain might not be able to take advantage of population increases if all of its outlets were placed in stagnant or declining locations.

> Note how the defense expert deftly exposed the flaws in the plaintiff's theory by concentrating on major issues, rather than picking out petty mistakes. Note also that the expert made no personal attacks. In essence, Dr. Isaacs took the high road, saying, "I have no personal quarrel with Dr. Lipton; she simply chose an inadequate theory."

6. Conclusion

An expert can expect the direct examination to conclude with counsel's request for an authoritative restatement of the most important conclusions.

D. Clarity and Credibility

As noted earlier, a lawyer's goal in direct examination is to concentrate the fact finder's attention on the witness. This is especially true in the case of experts, since the attorney hopes that the witness will be able to educate the judge or jury. The very structure of direct examination serves to focus even more on the witness, since the lawyer is more or less confined to short, open-ended questions.

An expert witness consequently has considerable latitude in framing her replies to questions on direct. Of course, the answers must be responsive to the questions, they must be relevant to the issues in the case, and they must consist of admissible evidence. Beyond that, however, the content, structure, organization, and length of the answer are all within the witness's control.

In answering questions, the experts should always strive for clarity and credibility. The following sections discuss some of the ways an expert can achieve those goals while answering questions on direct examination.

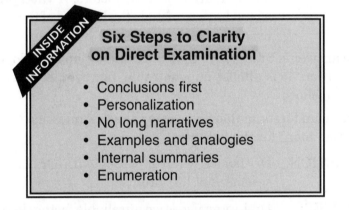

INSIDE INFORMATION

Six Steps to Clarity on Direct Examination

- Conclusions first
- Personalization
- No long narratives
- Examples and analogies
- Internal summaries
- Enumeration

Start with the conclusion!

1. Give Conclusions Before Explanations

Whenever possible, the format for an answer should be "conclusion first, then explanation." Although this approach is practically the opposite of most ordinary conversations, it is usually the best way to convey information while testifying in court.

In a casual discussion between friends, it is common to build up to one's conclusion: "I was out of bananas and my car was not working, so I put on my sneakers and jogged to the store." The pattern was appropriate for two reasons: (1) the information is simple and short, and (2) it is fairly certain that the listener will be interested in the explanation as well as the result.

In expert testimony, of course, neither of these premises holds true. The explanations are unlikely to be either simple or short and, more important, the fact finder needs the conclusion in order to understand the significance of the explanation itself. Unless the conclusion is given first, a fact finder may well wonder, "Where is all of this going?"

Here is what happens when an expert begins an answer by explaining:

QUESTION: Dr. Isaacs, what is wrong with Dr. Lipton's assessment of lost profits?

ANSWER: Vehicle miles are almost never spread uniformly across a state. They tend to increase much more in rural and suburban areas. Population, however, grows faster in the suburbs than in the countryside, and the urban growth rate has been surprisingly high lately. So it is really impossible to base a projection, as Dr. Lipton did, primarily on a combination of those factors. A valid projection would have to include the location of the plaintiff's existing restaurants.

The answer is coherent in that the explanation leads logically to the conclusion. It is almost impenetrable, however, because it is so difficult to follow.

A more understandable answer to the same question would provide a "road map" for the listener:

QUESTION: Dr. Isaacs, what is wrong with Dr. Lipton's assessment of lost profits?

ANSWER: Dr. Lipton used two unreliable factors in reaching her opinion, and she completely omitted the location of the existing restaurants—which is the most important factor of all. You can't depend on vehicle miles, as Dr. Lipton did, because they are almost never spread uniformly across a state. They tend to increase much more in rural and suburban areas. Population, however, grows faster in the suburbs than in the countryside, and the urban growth rate has been surprisingly high lately. So it is really impossible to base a projection primarily on a combination of those factors. A valid projection would have to include the location of the plaintiff's existing restaurants.

By starting with the conclusion, this answer provides a clear context for all of the explanatory facts.

Note that the "conclusion first" structure can be used for simple answers as well as complex ones. For example,

QUESTION: Dr. Lipton, what is the relationship between vehicle miles and profit projections?

ANSWER: Profits in the drive-in restaurant industry virtually always rise right along with vehicle miles. I looked at the government statistics for the last five years, and they show an extremely close correlation between miles driven in a state and fast-food revenues there.

Or,

QUESTION: In addition to your academic background, do you have any experience that has helped you form your opinion in this case?

ANSWER: Absolutely. My consulting work with major retailers gives me important insights into profit projection. For example, I have seen how the companies themselves use population statistics to plan expansion.

2. Personalization

Experts from academic, scientific, technical, or financial backgrounds may appear aloof, intimidating, or even arrogant to jurors who do not share their special training and expertise. This impediment to communication can be overcome through personalization.

Witnesses should understand the importance of allowing fact finders to get to know them as individuals, not just as authorities. In most jurisdictions lawyers are permitted to bring out a witness's personal and family background information and, within limits, to ask the witness about more than strictly professional matters. These questions should not be regarded as formalities or, worse, with a show of annoyance. Rather, the witness should understand that personalization is an essential aspect of establishing credibility.

Expert testimony does not have to be stiff and formal. A witness should not be afraid to illustrate her testimony with examples from everyday life or to refer to something in her own background in order to convey a point.

3. Plain Language

Virtually every field of expertise creates its own technical and shorthand terms. Expert witnesses are often inclined to use arcane and jargon-laden speech without even thinking about it. It is extremely important, however, for expert witnesses to learn how to testify in ordinary language. There are very few concepts that cannot be translated into plain speech.

Good lawyers understand the importance of simple language and will often ask for an explanation when an expert slips into her native tongue, whether it is finance-talk, engineeringese, or econo-speak. Such a request should be viewed as an opportunity, not a reprimand:

QUESTION: Dr. Longhini, do you have an opinion as to why the pressure plate failed?

ANSWER: Yes. My tests indicate that the fastening bolts were over-torqued.

QUESTION: What do you meant by "over-torqued?"

ANSWER: I mean that the bolts were turned too far when they were tightened.

The witness, however, should not depend on counsel to act as a translator. Too many lawyers, perhaps out of a desire to appear erudite themselves, tend to examine expert witnesses using the expert's own jargon. Such examinations can take on the characteristics of a private, and completely inaccessible, conversation between the lawyer and the witness. It is bad enough when attorneys use legalese among themselves; it is worse when they attempt to embrace the private speech of another profession. Consider the following:

QUESTION: Dr. Shiraishi, what injuries did you observe?

ANSWER: I observed multiple contusions on the anterior upper extremities.

QUESTION: Was there anything remarkable about the contusions?

ANSWER: Yes. They varied in color, which indicated that they had been inflicted at different times.

QUESTION: Did the anterior location of the contusions indicate anything further to you?

ANSWER: The anterior location on the upper extremities suggested that the contusions had been inflicted from a superior position.

The lawyer and doctor are talking about bruised arms. The witness began using the term "contusions" because it is medically precise, and the lawyer's adoption of the term encouraged the doctor to continue using it. Someone—lawyer or witness—will have to break this cozy cycle if the jury is ever to comprehend the significance of the injuries.

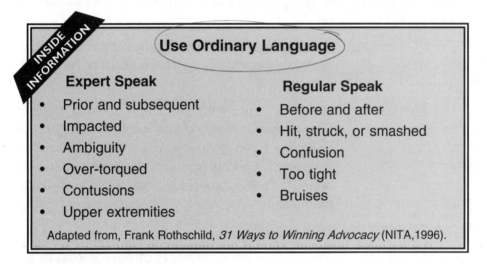

INSIDE INFORMATION

Use Ordinary Language

Expert Speak	**Regular Speak**
• Prior and subsequent	• Before and after
• Impacted	• Hit, struck, or smashed
• Ambiguity	• Confusion
• Over-torqued	• Too tight
• Contusions	• Bruises
• Upper extremities	

Adapted from, Frank Rothschild, *31 Ways to Winning Advocacy* (NITA, 1996).

4. Avoid Long Narratives

Most judges will allow expert witnesses considerable freedom to testify in narrative fashion, on the theory that narratives are necessary in order to convey complex information. Many lawyers believe that they should take advantage of this leeway, and they therefore encourage their experts to present their testimony in long, uninterrupted segments. This is a mistake. Narratives are hard to follow and hard to digest. The most understandable answers will be concise, perhaps no more than three or four sentences in length.

Anyone who ever sat through a long lecture or speech should understand how difficult it is to pay attention to a speaker for an extended period of time. This is especially true of expert testimony, which often concentrates on complex or intricate details. A long, unbroken stretch of expert testimony is little more than an invitation to juror inattention.

It has long been understood that an audience will remember best those things that they hear first. This principle, often called "primacy," applies equally to judges and jurors, and it obtains to individual answers as well as to entire examinations.

Reinitiating primacy and avoiding narratives ✳✳

A new answer begins every time counsel asks a question. Thus, every question to the expert reinitiates primacy and refocuses the fact finder's attention. A long, narrative answer, however, will have no comparable points of natural reinitiation. Unless the witness is an extraordinarily skilled speaker, the use of narratives will destroy one opportunity to highlight the examination's most important points.

In the following example, note how the attorney punctuates the testimony at logical breaking points. By avoiding narratives, the expert reinitiates primacy three times and emphasizes three important aspects of his opinion:

QUESTION: Dr. Isaacs, what is the significance of location in projecting profits for a chain of drive-in restaurants?

ANSWER: Location is probably the single most important factor when it comes to profitability in any retail business. Even if the overall trend in an industry is upward, a poorly located business is unlikely to benefit. This is especially true of the restaurant business.

QUESTION: Please explain.

ANSWER: The restaurant business is intensely local in nature. There are very few restaurants that attract people from great distances. Most people eat near their homes, their places of work, or their shopping destinations. So a restaurant in an undesirable neighborhood or in a declining business district simply will not draw customers.

QUESTION: Why is that?

ANSWER: Many restaurants depend heavily on luncheon trade. People on their lunch breaks usually do not have more than an hour, and often less. So a restaurant will not be able to draw this business unless it is located near a fairly large number of employers. No matter how well the economy is doing, a restaurant will not do well at lunchtime if it is located in an area that happens to have experienced a downturn.

Note that the answers above were not cut off and were not unnaturally short or truncated. The witness adequately explained each concept, but resisted the temptation to string all of the ideas together into a single, extended narrative.

5. Examples and Analogies

Many complex ideas can be made more understandable through the use of examples, analogies, or metaphors. Consider the following use of an example to flesh out a relatively abstract concept:

QUESTION: Dr. Isaacs, could you give us an example of how a restaurant chain might do poorly, even in a state with an expanding population and increasing vehicle miles?

ANSWER: Certainly. Many urban areas have experienced population growth that is basically limited to the suburbs. A restaurant chain that was concentrated in the central city would show almost no increased profitability as a result of that growth. In fact, its profits might well decline because of the population shift. That is why location is such an important factor.

An analogy could serve the same purpose:

QUESTION: Dr. Isaacs, could you please explain the importance of location a little further?

ANSWER: Well, maybe it would help to think about it this way. Imagine a baseball league with eight teams. If the two or three pennant contenders are all located in big cities, they will obviously draw a lot of fans. On the other hand, a cellar-dwelling team in a small city would probably play to an empty stadium. So even if the league's overall attendance went up, that wouldn't help to fill the seats for the last-place team. A poor location is a lot like being stuck in last place.

A witness should not depend on midtestimony inspiration to come up with analogies and metaphors. The time to consider explanatory imagery is during preparation, not on the spur of the moment in the midst of the direct examination.

6. Internal Summaries

Because of the potential length and complexity of expert testimony, it is often important to highlight significant points through the use of internal summaries. Think of expert testimony as containing a series of steps or elements. At the conclusion of each step it may be helpful for the expert to explain how he got there, why it is important, and where he is going next. Here is an example from the drive-in case:

QUESTION: Dr. Isaacs, please summarize your objections to Dr. Lipton's methodology.

ANSWER: The problem with Dr. Lipton's approach is that she failed to consider several of the most important factors in determining profitability. Her reliance on population and vehicle miles led her to dramatically overestimate the restaurant chain's likely profitability. Her study was especially deficient because it did not account for either location or potential competition.

QUESTION: Were you able to conduct a more comprehensive study?

ANSWER: Yes. I conducted a study that included the six most important factors, all of which were omitted by Dr. Lipton.

7. Enumeration

Audiences often pay closer attention to information presented in numbered lists. It can be useful, therefore, to introduce concepts in terms of factors or considerations rather than launching directly into extended explanations. The following is a good example of enumeration:

QUESTION: Dr. Isaacs, what is your opinion of Dr. Lipton's study?

ANSWER: There are three basic problems with Dr. Lipton's study.

QUESTION: What are those three problems?

ANSWER: First, she projected profits on the basis of only two factors. Second, she failed to consider location, which should have been the most important element. Third, she doesn't seem to recognize that population growth can be extremely uneven.

Following this summary, the expert can now proceed to explain each of the three points in detail. Note also that the introduction of each point will reinitiate primacy and therefore focus the fact finder's attention.

8. Consensus

Almost every field of expertise contains several contending schools of thought. Opposing experts often arrive at different opinions because they approach the issues from distinct perspectives. For example, a strict Freudian psychoanalyst is likely to evaluate a patient's mental state quite differently from a Gestalt therapist.

It may be important, therefore, to stress that a witness's point of view lies within the mainstream and that it is not a novel or untested theory. This can be done by highlighting university affiliation, professional certification, or other indicia of widespread acceptance.

The question of consensus can also be taken up directly:

QUESTION: Dr. Isaacs, what is the consensus view on the projection of retail business profits?

ANSWER: The strong consensus is that multiple factors have to be considered and that location is the single most important variable.

QUESTION: Is Dr. Lipton's method within that consensus?

ANSWER: No. Dr. Lipton basically tries to take a shortcut. She substitutes population growth for all other factors. I do not believe there is a single business school in the United States today that teaches students to project profits that way.

QUESTION: How do you know about the way business schools teach that subject?

ANSWER: My book, *Principles of Business Valuation,* is used at over forty business schools. So I know firsthand how those schools cover the topic, and I also read all of the other leading textbooks—sort of keeping an eye on the competition.

9. Powerful Language

When talking among themselves, professionals often adopt a tone of reserved judgment. It is not that they are uncertain, but rather that "open-mindedness" is an important goal or value. Thus, it is not uncommon to hear an expert hedge her opinion by saying something like "it seems to me under current circumstances," or "my best information suggests," or "at the moment I would have to say." In a professional setting, such language is not intended or understood as equivocal, but only as an acknowledgment that any conclusion may be subject to further inquiry.

The result can be very different in a courtroom, however. To prevent inadvertent miscommunication, experts should avoid using language that unintentionally hedges or qualifies their opinions, using wording instead that emphasizes accuracy and certainty.

Here is an example of weak language:

ANSWER: My best estimate at this time is that the restaurant chain would have earned approximately $3.2 million over the next five years.

In fact, the witness has conducted an exhaustive study and is completely certain, within the bounds of professional competence, that $3.2 million is the correct figure. That certainty can be better expressed through more powerful language:

ANSWER: I have calculated lost profits at $3.2 million.

Or,

ANSWER: My projections show that the restaurant chain would have earned $3.2 million over the next five years.

Or,

ANSWER: The result of my study is a determination of lost profits in the amount of $3.2 million.

Of course, if the conclusions really are tentative or provisional, the witness should not testify otherwise.

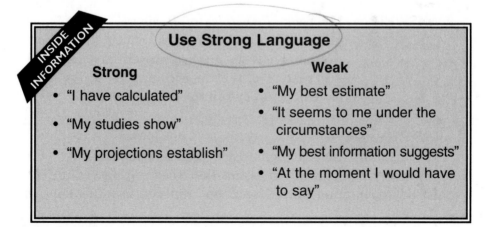

INSIDE INFORMATION

Use Strong Language

Strong
- "I have calculated"
- "My studies show"
- "My projections establish"

Weak
- "My best estimate"
- "It seems to me under the circumstances"
- "My best information suggests"
- "At the moment I would have to say"

10. Do Not Stretch Expertise

It may be tempting to attempt to stretch one's expertise, either at the invitation of retaining counsel or in response to cross-examination. In either situation, this is a misguided undertaking. It is risky, in extreme cases bordering on unethical, to testify beyond one's legitimate field.

In the restaurant scenario we have seen examples of testimony from financial experts on the question of lost profits. As we have imagined the plaintiff's expert, she was called and qualified solely with regard to the issue of damages. Some attorneys, however, might attempt to have the witness offer an opinion on liability as well. Perhaps the witness might do double duty by testifying that the defendant's pricing practices were predatory.

There are two immediate problems with this approach. First, it is unlikely that a single economist would really possess expertise with regard both to damage modeling and pricing practices. Second, even assuming sufficient expertise, once this witness takes a position on liability she may be compromised as an impartial arbiter of damages. A witness who advances too many favorable opinions may soon come to be seen as a shill or hired gun.

11. Visual Aids

The direct examination of almost every expert can be enhanced through the use of visual displays. Since expert testimony is often hard to follow, it may be particularly important to portray many of the concepts with charts, graphs, drawings, or models.

A physician's testimony, for example, can be brought to life with an anatomical model or series of colored overlays. Financial experts should illustrate their testimony with graphs or tables. An architectural or engineering expert should use diagrams or scale models. The possibilities for visual aids are practically infinite, limited only by the expert's imagination.

Two cautions. First, unless the witness is also an actual expert at drawing or model construction, it is preferable to obtain professional assistance in developing visual displays. Second, the expert should understand that visual aids will have to be marked as exhibits in the case, and perhaps offered and admitted into evidence. Although the displays are used to convey the expert's testimony, they are also, by definition, part of counsel's case. There may be legal or procedural rules that govern their use, or there may be other reasons to restrict or elaborate on a particular exhibit. Thus, visual aids should not be created by the expert alone, but always in consultation with retaining counsel.

E. Objections

(margin note: Include in workshop on expert testimony)

1. The Role of Objections at Trial

An objection is nothing more than a request from one of the attorneys that the court rule on the admissibility of certain testimony or evidence. The purpose of objecting is to prevent the introduction or consideration of inadmissible information. Although the process of objecting has become associated in the popular mind with contentiousness and even hostility, that need not be the case. Our adversary system relies upon opposing attorneys to present evidence and the judge to decide upon its admissibility. An objection, then, is simply a signal to the judge that there is a disagreement between counsel concerning the rules of evidence or procedure.

When there are no objections, which is the overwhelming majority of the time, the judge can allow evidence to come into the record without the need for a specific ruling. If we had no process of objecting, the trial judge would have to rule upon every separate answer and item of evidence. Unless the process is abused or misused, trials are actually expedited by the judge's ability to rely upon counsel to object to questionable evidence.

2. Types of Objections

Objections may be made to an attorney's questions, to a witness's testimony, to the introduction or use of exhibits, to a lawyer's demeanor or behavior, to the conduct of the judge, or to virtually anything else that occurs at trial.

An attorney's question may be objectionable because of its form or because it calls for inadmissible evidence. A question is objectionable as to form when it seeks to obtain information in an impermissible way. For example, a leading question on direct examination is improper because it tells the witness what answer is expected. Even if the answer itself would be admissible, the question is disallowed because of its suggestiveness. Compound questions, vague questions, and argumentative questions, to name a few, are also objectionable as to form.

A question phrased in proper form might nonetheless call for inadmissible evidence. The information sought may be irrelevant, privileged, or hearsay. An objection may be made when it is apparent from the question itself that the answer should not be admitted. For example, the question, "What is your religious belief?" is in proper form on either direct or cross-examination. Any answer, however, would be inadmissible under most circumstances by virtue of the Federal Rules of Evidence.[7]

Even in the absence of an objectionable question, a witness may respond with an inadmissible answer. The answer might volunteer irrelevant information, it might contain unanticipated hearsay, or it might consist entirely of speculation. For example, a direct examiner could ask the perfectly allowable question, "How do you know that the restaurant chain would have realized $3.2 million in profits?" only to receive the hearsay reply, "Because the president of the company told me that is what his projections showed." Opposing counsel would no doubt object to the answer and move that it be stricken from the record.

3. Objections During Direct Examination

It is likely that there will be objections at one time or another during most direct examinations. When an objection is made, the appropriate response of the witness is ordinarily to sit quietly until it is ruled upon—the objection will be either sustained or denied, and the examination will then proceed. There are a few circumstances in which the witness may need to pay more careful attention to the lawyers' objections and responses.

Some attorneys tout the use of so-called "tactical" objections. This vexatious practice is intended to break up the flow of a successful examination by interposing a series of meaningless or ill-founded objections. Objections of this sort are made in order to throw the direct examiner off stride, confuse the witness, or distract the jury. Tactical objections are an unfortunate fact of life at trial, since most practitioners of this low art seem capable of giving some veneer of legitimacy to the constant interruptions. A witness who is being subjected to this tactic should respond by redoubling attention to the direct examiner. Eventually, most judges will realize what is going on and put at least a temporary stop to the harassment. Until then, the witness's best defense to tactical objections is to make sure that they do not interfere with her concentration.

---

7. Evidence of the beliefs or opinions of a witness on matters of religion is not admissible for the purpose of showing that by reason of their nature his credibility is impaired or enhanced. Rule 610, Federal Rules of Evidence. There may be other circumstances in which a witness's religious beliefs would be relevant to a case and therefore admissible in evidence.

When an objection is made to a question on direct examination, it is the lawyer's job to fix the problem or go on to another inquiry. The witness only needs to listen to the next question, and answer it if there is no further objection. Sometimes, however, the objection is to the witness's own answer. This can occur because the direct examiner has requested something flatly inadmissible. It may also be the case, however, that the witness's phrasing or word choice, and not the substance of the answer, lies at the heart of the problem

A witness, of course, should never guess at the reasons an objection has been sustained. Nor should a witness take the initiative in correcting a perceived problem with an answer. Rather, the witness should listen carefully to instructions that might come from the direct examiner or the judge. For example:

QUESTION: Dr. Shiraishi, do you have an opinion as to how the bruises were formed on the upper parts of the victim's arms?

ANSWER: Yes, Dr. Middleton told me that . . .

OPPOSING
COUNSEL: Objection. Hearsay.

THE COURT: Sustained.

QUESTION: Dr. Shiraishi, could you please give us your opinion without referring to anything someone else might have told you?

The instruction or direction might also come from the judge, especially if the witness is having trouble getting it right:

THE COURT: Dr. Shiraishi, at this point in the trial we are only interested in what you know from your own personal knowledge. So please answer the question strictly in terms of what you saw and did.

ANSWER: Certainly. My examination of the bruises indicated that they were inflicted from above while the victim had his arms raised. Based on my experience as a pathologist, I would call those "defense wounds."

The court and counsel may be helpful to the witness, telling her how the testimony must be phrased. The court may also give a witness strict instructions about what to omit:

QUESTION: Dr. Isaacs, why do you believe that the plaintiff's plans for expansion have been overstated?

ANSWER: I reviewed certain documents from the plaintiff's own records that . . .

OPPOSING
COUNSEL: Objection. The court has already ruled that those documents cannot be used at trial.[8]

THE COURT: Sustained. Dr. Isaacs, I have already granted what we call a "motion in limine," ruling that those documents are privileged and cannot be used at trial. You can continue your testimony, but you may not make any mention or use of the documents in question.

Such instructions from the court must be followed to the letter. A witness should not attempt to blurt out prohibited information or slip it in "through the back door."

F. Redirect Examination

Following direct examination, the witness will be tendered to opposing counsel for cross-examination.[9] Although cross-examination is not required, it is almost unheard of for an expert witness not to be questioned by the opposing party. Following cross-examination, the direct examiner may be given an opportunity to ask further questions—this is called redirect examination.

On redirect, the witness may be asked to explain points that were explored during the cross, to untangle seeming inconsistencies, to correct errors or misstatements, or to rebut new claims or inferences. In other words, an attorney's goal during redirect is to minimize or undo any damage that may have been effected during the cross-examination.

The material that can be covered on redirect is technically limited to the "scope" of the cross. The interpretation of this rule varies from court to court; some are quite strict and others are fairly lenient. Almost all courts, however, insist that the redirect must always have some reasonable relationship to matters that were raised on cross.

---

8. For the sake of brevity, we have omitted the process of marking and identifying the subject documents.

9. See Chapters Five, Six, and Seven.

The witness, therefore, can be fairly certain that there will be no questions on redirect concerning wholly new issues.

It is most likely that redirect examination will consist primarily of explanations and clarifications; the witness may also be asked to "complete" testimony that may have been cut off (fairly or unfairly) by the cross-examiner:

QUESTION: Dr. Lipton, the cross-examination suggested three times that you failed to consider location in calculating lost profits. Do you recall the cross?

ANSWER: I certainly do.

QUESTION: I'd like to give you an opportunity to explain. Did you consider location?

ANSWER: Yes, I did consider location. It was not a separate aspect of my projection, though, because the chain had statewide expansion plans. Thus, the separate locations of the individual outlets did not matter, since I used statewide figures for all my projections.

Note that redirect examination may be followed by recross, which may be followed by additional redirect, more recross, another redirect, and so on into the night. Each further examination is limited to the scope of the one that immediately preceded it. It is within the court's discretion to cut off re-examinations; there is no right to an infinite regression. Most judges routinely allow at least one redirect and one recross.

— Chapter Five —

CROSS-EXAMINATION—THE BASICS

A. Introduction

In this chapter we will discuss the basic concept of cross-examination itself. What is the lawyer seeking to achieve? What is the witness's actual role?

In brief, the lawyer's goal is almost always to embellish his case by controlling the witness's testimony. In contrast, the witness's objective is essentially to continue teaching—just as she did on direct examination.

This is the first of three chapters on cross-examination. The next two chapters cover attorneys' common techniques and approaches for conducting cross-examination (Chapter Six) and ways that witnesses can cope (Chapter Seven).

> **INSIDE INFORMATION**
>
> **Lawyers' Goals on Cross-Examination**
>
> - Control scope of witness's answers
> - Tell counsel's story
> - Minimize expert's impact
> - Limit expert's input

B. Lawyer's Goal—Control

The very thought of cross-examination often evokes images of antagonism and even hostility; the glaring attorney accuses the witness of ineptitude, indiscretion, malfeasance, or worse. The reality of cross-examination, particularly for expert witnesses, is typically less threatening and almost always less dramatic. There may occasionally be a spirited confrontation between lawyer and witness, but that situation is the exception not the rule.

From the witness's perspective, a lawyer's goals in the typical cross-examination of an expert may seem relatively modest. From the attorney's standpoint, however, the objectives of expert cross can be crucial or even case-breaking. The difference in perception arises because most of the lawyer's ends can be achieved without necessarily "shaking" or even appearing to challenge the gist of the expert's opinion. Many of the best, most effective cross-examinations turn out to be subtle indeed.

> The starting point in understanding cross-examination is an appreciation of the lawyer's most likely goals, of which there are three.

LAWYER'S GOALS IN CROSS

1. Telling Counsel's Story

A lawyer's first objective on cross-examination is to tell his client's story, using the witness only as a sounding board. In the ideal cross-examination, the lawyer is the narrator and the witness is simply along for the ride.

In the previous chapter we recognized that the witness is the center of attention on direct examination. The lawyer wants to tell a logical and dynamic story, but he must convey it exclusively through the narrative of the witness. This is so for two reasons. First, the law of direct examination limits the attorney to open-ended, nonleading questions. Thus, the lawyer may request information but cannot provide it. Second, particularly in regard to expert testimony, the direct examiner depends upon the witness's own credibility to support the case. The lawyer, therefore, wants to make the witness the "star" of the show.

In cross-examination, however, the considerations are virtually reversed.

The law of cross-examination allows the attorney to ask leading questions. A leading question is one that contains its own answer, meaning that it must be question in form only. In reality, most leading questions are factual propositions—the witness being asked only to agree or disagree. At the same time, the cross-examiner has little or no interest in preserving the opposing expert's credibility, or even allowing the witness to communicate in her own words. Thus, the cross-examiner can fashion a string of interrogative statements into a factual narrative that "leads" the witness through the desired story.

In the drive-in restaurant example, the defendant's expert testified on direct that "location is probably the single most important factor when it comes to profitability in any retail business." On cross-examination, plaintiff's counsel will want to use leading questions to tell a counterstory:

QUESTION: Restaurants can succeed in less than perfect locations, can't they?

ANSWER: Yes.

QUESTION: And locations can actually get better as the market changes, correct?

ANSWER: That can happen.

QUESTION: Of course, many chains compete for spots in the best locations, don't they?

ANSWER: They do.

QUESTION: And that results in lots of competition in those locations, correct?

ANSWER: Of course.

QUESTION: We all have seen four or five fast-food joints clustered together on the same strip, right?

ANSWER: That's right.

QUESTION: And those places are all competing for the same traffic, aren't they?

ANSWER: More or less.

QUESTION: So a somewhat less desirable location would have less competition, right?

ANSWER: Probably.

QUESTION: A smart operator might see that as an opportunity—you can't rule that out, can you?

ANSWER: No, I can't rule that out.

Note that each "question" was actually a statement of fact, and that each was more or less undeniable. The cross-examiner's theory is built up carefully, as the witness has little choice but to agree with each proposition. Slowly it emerges that the expert's "poor locations" can also be regarded as an entrepreneur's opportunity. The cross-examiner's story has been told.

---

2. Minimizing the Expert's Impact

Storytelling on cross-examination is an important technique for lawyers, but it is only as good as the story being told. Although the content of expert cross-examination will vary tremendously, a constant component is the minimization of the witness's direct. The lawyer may not attempt to "demolish" the expert, but he will almost certainly hope to diminish or reduce the impact of the expert's testimony.

Again, a good cross-examiner will rely almost exclusively on leading questions:

QUESTION: Many factors go into making a successful restaurant chain, correct?

ANSWER: Yes.

QUESTION: Price, quality, visibility, advertising, comfort—these things can all make a difference, can't they?

ANSWER: They can.

QUESTION: Location is an important factor, but it is only one factor among many, correct?

ANSWER: Yes.

QUESTION: Now, you are critical of Dr. Lipton for not adequately considering location, is that right?

ANSWER: Yes, I am.

QUESTION: But her study did include an analysis of the chain's advertising budget, didn't it?

ANSWER: It did.

QUESTION: It is possible for advertising to compensate for an inconvenient location, isn't that right?

ANSWER: That can happen.

QUESTION: Dr. Lipton also considered the chain's pricing policies, didn't she?

ANSWER: She did.

QUESTION: Low prices can also compensate for location, true?

ANSWER: Sometimes.

QUESTION: So you would have to agree that Dr. Lipton considered at least two factors that might offset the "location issue," correct?

ANSWER: She did consider those factors.

QUESTION: And the relative importance of those factors is a matter of judgment, isn't it?

ANSWER: I suppose it is.

QUESTION: Well, let me put it this way. You can't deny that in some situations advertising and pricing could be more important than location?

ANSWER: It would depend upon the situation.

QUESTION: And in this situation, you and Dr. Lipton happen to disagree, correct?

ANSWER: We disagree.

Without asking the witness to contradict himself or retract his testimony, the cross-examiner has led the witness away from one of his most important conclusions—that Dr. Lipton did not adequately consider location. The witness has now agreed that "in some situations," pricing and advertising might be more important. Thus, the firm disapproval of Dr. Lipton's testimony has been reduced to a matter of differing judgment.

3. Controlling the Expert's Input

Every competent trial lawyer understands that cross-examination is never the time to look for information. The lawyer doesn't want to learn anything, he merely wants to tell his story. Hence, the revered admonition, "Never ask a question if you don't know the answer."

In brief, the last thing a cross-examiner wants to hear is an actual answer—other than yes or no—from an expert witness. From the lawyer's perspective, a failed cross-examination is one in which the witness has been given an opportunity to explain. When all goes well for the attorney, the witness's role will be little more than monosyllabic agreement.

To achieve this end, lawyers have developed a variety of forensic devices for limiting a witness's ability to explain her answers. Experts will want to be familiar with the techniques of cross-examination, if only to increase their own understanding of the process. As the above examples make clear, the lawyer's principal, and extremely potent, tool is the leading question. In addition, there are three further methods used by attorneys to control the testimony of witnesses on cross-examination.

a. Incremental Questions

The larger the scope of a question, even a leading question, the more likely it is that a witness will find room to disagree or explain. Consequently, the most skilled cross-examinations proceed in a series of short, steady steps, with each area of questioning divided into its smallest component parts.

The lawyer in the fast-food case probably would not ask this question in cross-examining the plaintiff's witness:

QUESTION: Dr. Lipton, you did not consider the importance of location when you projected future profits, correct?

The broad scope of the question, leading as it is, gives the witness far too much latitude to deny or quibble. Incremental questions solve the attorney's problem:

QUESTION: Dr. Lipton, you based your projections on two primary factors, correct?

QUESTION: You concentrated on those factors because you thought they were the most important ones, didn't you?

QUESTION: The first factor was population growth, right?

QUESTION: And the second factor involved vehicle miles, correct?

QUESTION: Population growth has nothing to do with a restaurant's location, does it?

QUESTION: Same thing for vehicle miles, right?

b. Sequenced Questions

The order of the questions can be as important as their content. Lawyers control witnesses through the use of sequencing, beginning with the most undeniable aspects of the examination and proceeding to more difficult areas only once the groundwork has been laid.

With expert witnesses, the sequencing often proceeds from general to specific, with the witness first being asked to agree with a very expansive statement of principle. Recall that the defendant's expert in the restaurant case testified that poor location doomed the plaintiff's business to a bleak economic future:

QUESTION: Dr. Isaacs, will you agree with me that within any given industry, the profitability of individual companies can vary dramatically?

QUESTION: Some companies make money and others show losses?

QUESTION: And the difference between making money and losing it is often a matter of efficient management?

QUESTION: Good management can cope with a variety of difficult circumstances, correct?

QUESTION: And bad management can fail, even if all the other indicators are positive, right?

QUESTION: So when you get right down to it, generalities may not matter as much as management, right?

QUESTION: Now when you say that location is the most important thing—that's a generality, isn't it?

The sequencing in this example was essential. Everything was built upon the expert's initial agreement that "the profitability of different companies can vary dramatically."

c. Absence of Ultimate Questions

Expert witnesses often find that cross-examinations seem strangely incomplete. The lawyer uses a series of short, leading, sequenced, incremental questions, all of which seem directed to a certain conclusion—but the *ultimate* question is never asked. In the first example above, it certainly seems as though the lawyer should go on to ask something like

QUESTION: So, it is true that you did not consider the importance of location when you projected future profits, correct?

In the second example we also expect the lawyer to continue on to the conclusion:

QUESTION: So location might not be so important after all, right?

Why won't the lawyer go all the way? The reason is that counsel does not want to surrender control of the cross-examination. The leading, sequenced, incremental questions are all designed to constrain the expert's answers, steering the witness inexorably in the desired direction. Asking the final question, however, invites the witness to disagree or (horrors!) to explain—and explanation is the last thing a cross-examiner ever wants to hear.

Thus, astute cross-examiners almost always make the ultimate point by implication. In the above examples, for instance, it should be completely obvious where the examinations are headed. Asking the final question would not make the message any more apparent, it would just allow the witness an opportunity to hedge or retract. And if the innuendo really needs to be clarified, the lawyer can always accomplish that during final argument—after the witness has been excused and is no longer able to respond.

INSIDE INFORMATION

Cross-Examination Techniques

Incremental questions: Short, steady steps, with each area of questioning divided into its smallest component parts.

Sequenced questions: Begins with the most undeniable aspects and proceeds to the difficult areas once the attorney has laid the groundwork.

No ultimate questions: Astute cross-examiners make the ultimate point by implication; denies the witness an opportunity to explain.

C. Witness's Perspective—Teach and Explain

Much as the cross-examiner may want the witness to function merely as a sounding board, an expert actually has a much broader part to play on cross-examination.

The witness's first priority is to be as cooperative as the cross-examiner allows. Cross-examination is a necessary and important part of the justice system. Although it may be discomfiting to have one's opinion tested, the challenges are usually fair and respectful. Witnesses should not take cross-examination personally—unless, of course, the attorney makes it personal. Certainly, a witness should not attempt to thwart or impede the cross-examination. Fair questions deserve fair answers.

To be sure, some cross-examinations are unprincipled or even nasty; lawyers may resort to deception and trickery. Some lawyers deliberately set out to shake the witness's composure through harassment and intimidation. To the extent possible, however, a witness should not allow such tactics to interfere with her function on the stand. As discussed below, most of counsel's provocative techniques can be dealt with quite handily through cooperation, education, integrity, and explanation.[1]

1. Cooperation and Education

Other than in cases of overt provocation by the attorney, an uncooperative witness tends to diminish her own credibility. Lawyers understand this dynamic and often attempt to exploit it through a series of ploys designed to make the witness seem uncooperative. And some witnesses, it must be said, appear to lose their cool with little if any encouragement from counsel.

An expert witness can usually remain cooperative by remembering that her primary function is educational. She is in court in order to be a teacher, to convey information. An intransigent cross-examiner might best be regarded as a somewhat difficult student—steady explanation, rather than exasperation or resentment, is probably the preferable approach.

It will help in this regard for the expert to bear in mind that the cross-examiner is not really the intended recipient of the information. The witness wants to communicate with the judge or jury; the lawyers are only incidental to the process. In particular, the cross-examiner is actually assigned the job of disagreeing with the witness's conclusions. A lawyer will virtually never stop cross-examining and say, "Oh yes, now I understand; you are quite right after all."

Thus, if the witness's conclusions are clear and well supported, there is no need to worry if the cross-examiner is feigning confusion or disbelief. The witness is there for the benefit of the fact finder, not the opposing attorney.

2. Integrity

A witness's primary concern on cross-examination should be maintaining the integrity of her opinion. The word integrity comes from the Latin *integritas,* meaning wholeness or soundness, complete in itself. An expert witness expresses an opinion because it is accurate, sound, principled—not because it will help a lawyer win a case.

---

1. Some more specific coping mechanisms are discussed in Chapter Seven.

The witness's goal, therefore, is to explain and support the opinion, not to defend it at all cost and certainly not to "defeat" the cross-examiner. An expert should be prepared and willing to answer all questions, whether reasonable or silly, legitimate or ill-founded.

The best answers will often refer back to the expert's theory, explaining *why* the expert chose her approach and *why* that approach yields a reliable answer. An expert who is confident in her theory will also be confident in the integrity of her opinion. She will be able to answer sensible questions intelligently and to respond patiently to foolish ones. Nor should the expert fear making concessions. A competent cross-examiner may ask for any number of sound, reasonable concessions from a witness, and those requests should never be fought simply for the sake of foiling the examination.

3. Explanation

It is well and good to say that an expert witness should cooperate and teach while defending the integrity of her opinion. But how is the witness to do that while the cross-examiner is making a well-oiled effort to confine and control every answer?

We have seen that a cross-examiner's purpose in life is to control the flow of testimony on cross-examination. While an expert does not exactly want to wrest control of the examination away from the lawyer, the witness does want to protect her ability to function as something more than the proverbial potted plant. In other words, the witness wants to ensure a measure of independence from the complete management of the cross-examiner.

The key lies in explanation. An expert witness must be alert for opportunities or invitations to explain her answers. This does not mean, of course, that the witness should attempt to disrupt the cross-examination by interjecting explanations at every turn. Quite the contrary, a witness should be content to answer "yes or no" when such an answer will be fair and complete. On other hand, the witness must realize that sometimes an explanation is essential and that it may take some initiative to be allowed to provide one.

The following sections detail some of the opportunities an expert witness may be given to explain answers on cross-examination.

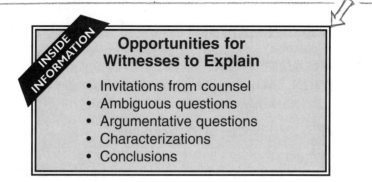

Opportunities for Witnesses to Explain

INSIDE INFORMATION

- Invitations from counsel
- Ambiguous questions
- Argumentative questions
- Characterizations
- Conclusions

a. Invitations

Though cross-examiners are well advised to ask only short, leading, incremental questions, many fail at the task. Most cross-examiners, either occasionally or constantly, will no doubt ask questions that virtually solicit explanation from the witness. An attentive witness will recognize these situations and accept the invitation.

The clearest invitations are straightforward. Though it breaks all of the "rules" of cross-examination, some attorneys cannot restrain themselves from requesting explanations, even when they start with tight, leading questions. Whatever the form of the invitation, there is only one appropriate response:

QUESTION: Dr. Lipton, your approach to damages relied primarily on population growth and vehicle miles, correct?

ANSWER: Yes, that is correct.

QUESTION: You did not specifically consider the location of the plaintiff's individual restaurants, right?

ANSWER: I did not look at specific locations.

QUESTION: You realize, from Dr. Isaacs's report, that location is closely related to profitability?

ANSWER: I understand that.

QUESTION: How can you explain the fact that you did not look at the individual locations?

ANSWER: I will be glad to explain.

A "why" question also invites explanation:

QUESTION: Why did you use population growth and vehicle miles instead of location when you projected profits?

ANSWER: I will be glad to explain.

Or the question could be slightly more hostile:

QUESTION: What makes you think you can project profits without considering location?

ANSWER: I will be glad to explain.

A well-prepared expert witness will have a ready answer for the cross-examiner when asked to explain some part of her opinion.

b. Ambiguous Questions

Among lawyers, it is a well known cross-examination technique to plant an ambiguity in the middle of a question, on the theory that it will slide right past the witness. After the witness affirms the answer, the lawyer can exploit the ambiguity, either in following questions or during final argument. Questions of this sort pose a problem for the witness, since she will not want to seem recalcitrant about answering apparently reasonable questions. Nor will the witness want to argue with counsel about the suitability or fairness of the question, since the ambiguities may be quite subtle.

The best response, therefore, is often to treat the question as one that calls for a brief explanation. In the following example, an expert physician has testified about injuries to a child. Note the ambiguity in the cross-examiner's questions:

QUESTION: Dr. Shiraishi, you observed bruises that varied in color, correct?

ANSWER: Yes, I did.

QUESTION: Color variation is a meaningful difference, right?

ANSWER: That is correct.

QUESTION: Color variation indicates a disparity in the infliction of the injuries, doesn't it?

The word "disparity" is the crowning, and quite intentional, ambiguity. The witness might understand it to mean one thing, though it can actually be interpreted in many different ways. If the witness just accepts the term, the lawyer will no doubt exploit the "disparity," perhaps by arguing that the injuries were inflicted by several different people or in an accident.

Instead, the witness can use the ambiguous question as an opportunity for a short explanation:

ANSWER: Color variation tells me that the bruises were inflicted over a fairly long period of time, but there is no disparity in the way they were received.

c. Argumentative Questions

Expert witnesses often feel intimidated by overbearing or argumentative questions. They imply that the witness made a mistake or that the lawyer is about to clobber the witness with some hidden fact or stunning revelation. Though the possibility of expert error should never be discounted, intimidating questions are often asked more for effect than anything else.

Argumentative questions can frequently be recognized by their "yet still" format, which often indicates that the cross-examiner cares more about coercion than content. In these situations, explanation can serve as a ready antidote to intimidation.

Return to the restaurant example:

QUESTION: Location can be an extremely important factor in the success of a restaurant, correct?

ANSWER: That is correct.

QUESTION: Some restaurant chains even hire consultants to help them evaluate locations, right?

ANSWER: Yes, they do.

QUESTION: *Yet still,* you insisted on looking at population growth and vehicle miles, didn't you?

In words and sarcasm, the cross-examiner hopes to imply that there was something questionable about the expert's choice. A simple "yes" might suggest acceptance of the innuendo, but an explanation will defuse it.

ANSWER: I based my analysis on population growth because the chain's locations were spread evenly around the entire state and I was able to use statewide figures for all of my projections.

The argumentative question may also take the "you still" form:

QUESTION: *And you still* claim that you can project profits on the basis of vehicle miles and population growth?

A meek "Yes I do" will seem defensive at best. At worst, it will be interpreted as a concession that the expert's calculation was only a "claim." It will be tempting to argue back, but note how that will only aggravate the situation by making the witness seem quarrelsome or uncooperative:

ANSWER: It isn't just a claim.

QUESTION: You say it isn't a claim, *but you still* want us to believe that you can base a projection on miles or population?

By engaging in argument, the witness has given the lawyer an opportunity to ask a trick question. Consider the limited possibilities: "Yes, I do still want you to believe it," or "No, I don't still want you to believe it." At this point, either answer plays right into the cross-examiner's hands.

The better response to the original question would have been a concise explanation, rather than an argument:

QUESTION: *And you still* claim that you can project profits on the basis of vehicle miles and population growth?

ANSWER: Profits are directly related to vehicle miles because the drive-in restaurants were evenly distributed throughout the state.

d. Characterizations and Conclusions

Invitations to explain may also arise when the cross-examiner resorts to characterizations or conclusions. A cross-examiner exercises the most control when the questions are limited to propositions of bedrock fact—the witness must then either agree or look foolish. The more a question strays from fact, the more latitude the witness is given to explain.

Imagine an ordinary cross-examination. The witness observed a street crime that occurred in the late evening, and the attorney wants to challenge his ability to identify the defendant. The examination will probably work as long as the lawyer sticks to facts:

QUESTION: The crime occurred on March 19, correct?

ANSWER: Yes, it did.

QUESTION: It happened at around 9:00 P.M., right?

ANSWER: Right, it was just about 9:00.

QUESTION: The sun had gone down hours earlier, right?

ANSWER: Probably at a little after 6:00 P.M.

So far, so good. The witness is under control, and the point is made. The lawyer might even want to gild the lily, though pretty much sticking with facts:

QUESTION: The cars were using their headlights, weren't they?

ANSWER: I think they were.

QUESTION: And that's because it was already dark, correct?

ANSWER: Yes.

Now watch what happens when the attorney switches from facts to characterizations:

QUESTION: So it was too dark to see clearly, wasn't it?

ANSWER: That's not right—I could see his face clearly by the light of the street lamps.

The conclusory question—"it was too dark to see?"—virtually asked the witness to spell out just how he was able to identify the defendant.

It works the same way with experts. An imbedded characterization or conclusion is really an open invitation to explain. Let us take another look at the restaurant case, classifying a series of questions as either factual or conclusory. Within the context of the testimony, the following question is based on fact; a reasonable witness cannot quibble:

QUESTION: Location can be an extremely important factor in the success of a restaurant, correct?

ANSWER: That is correct.

The next question asks for another fact, with which the witness will have to agree:

QUESTION: Some restaurant chains even hire consultants to help them evaluate locations, right?

ANSWER: Yes, they do.

But the next question calls for a conclusion, and that allows the witness to explain:

QUESTION: And that is because location is more important than anything else, isn't it?

ANSWER: For a statewide restaurant chain, the distribution of outlets is more important than any single location, since visibility and reliability are factors that bring people into the restaurants; so I would have to disagree with you.

✳✳ Note that the witness clearly took the role of the lawyer's teacher and did not answer as an adversary. The witness accomplished this for three reasons: (1) The explanation was succinct; (2) it was not contentious; and (3) it truly answered the question.

— Chapter Six —

CROSS-EXAMINATION—WHAT TO EXPECT

A. Introduction

Many experts are wary of cross-examination because they do not know what to expect. Realizing that the process is largely out of their control, witnesses worry about the implications of every question and answer.

Knowledge, however, is empowering. Much of the witness's anxiety can be overcome simply by understanding the operation of cross-examination. What comes first? How will it proceed? Why are they asking those questions?

This chapter begins by outlining just how lawyers themselves prepare for cross-examination and then goes on to explain the seven most common cross-examination techniques. The next chapter discusses ways that witnesses can cope with cross-examination.

B. Lawyer's Preparation

A good lawyer will be well prepared to cross-examine an expert witness. Often this will mean that the lawyer has conducted a thorough investigation of the technical aspects of the testimony. Many lawyers claim that, for the limited purposes of cross-examination, they virtually become experts themselves in the relevant field. Of course, some lawyers are better at this than others. It is not unusual for an expert to be confronted by an attorney who possesses dangerously little knowledge, but who persists in tormenting the expert with a series of ill-informed, pretentious questions.

On the other hand, quite a few lawyers succeed admirably at educating themselves in the expert's field. Of course, no medical malpractice attorney could ever actually treat a patient or perform a procedure, but many become quite adept at discussing the diagnostic or therapeutic alternatives available to practicing physicians.

It would be an arrogant mistake for an expert to assume that no cross-examiner will be able to challenge her knowledge or judgment.

Cross-examination is an art, and the best practitioners will understand exactly how to undermine an expert's opinion by using information from her own discipline. In short, an expert witness must expect to have her expertise tested on cross-examination.

The lawyer's research will often extend beyond the expert's subject matter and into the witness's own professional background. An expert should assume that the cross-examiner has read everything she has ever published. An enterprising lawyer will also have obtained any transcripts of the expert's previous trial or deposition testimony, in the hope of being able to impeach the witness with her own prior statements.

The cross-examiner may also have investigated the expert's professional affiliations, past clients, governmental positions, and other associations. Many experts have become closely associated with certain positions or attitudes (or clients) over the course of their careers, and it is fair game to raise this on cross-examination.

In addition, the cross-examination of an expert witness will usually utilize one or more of the following techniques, often in the order given below.

C. Challenging Credentials

If an expert's qualifications are to be challenged, it will typically happen at the very beginning of the cross-examination, or even earlier. An expert witness's credentials may be questioned at two different points in the trial—voir dire and cross-examination.

1. Voir Dire on Credentials

Voir dire is a limited cross-examination that temporarily suspends the direct so that the opposing attorney may inquire into the expert's qualifications. Once the proponent of an expert has concluded the qualification segment of the direct examination, opposing counsel is entitled to conduct a "voir dire." The direct examination is actually interrupted, and the cross-examiner is allowed to inquire into the expert's education, training, background, and preparation.

In essence, the voir dire is a mini-cross, aimed exclusively at the legal sufficiency of the expert's qualifications. In legal terms, the only question is whether the witness is "qualified as an expert by knowledge, skill, experience, training, or education."[1] No matter what the

---

1. Rule 702, Federal Rules of Evidence.

voir dire uncovers, the witness will usually be allowed to proceed with her testimony so long as she meets this minimum requirement.

Though it is fairly unusual, it is possible for an expert to be barred from testifying following an effective voir dire. Purported experts can be disqualified by establishing the remoteness of their credentials, the inapplicability of their specialties, the lack of general acceptance of their claimed expertise, or the unreliability of their data.

Voir dire concerns only the legal sufficiency of the expert's opinion, not its weight or persuasiveness. Consequently, voir dire is often (though not always) conducted outside the presence of the jury.

2. Cross-Examination on Credentials

The court's ruling that a witness may testify as an expert means only that the witness possesses sufficient credentials to pass the evidentiary threshold. Opposing counsel may still attempt to diminish the weight of the expert's qualifications during cross-examination. Lawyers use three basic methods for discrediting an expert.

a. Limiting the Scope of a Witness's Expertise

Although a witness may be well qualified in a certain area or subspecialty, it may be possible to recast the issues of the case in such a way as to place them beyond the bounds of the witness's competence. Assume, for example, that the plaintiff's expert in the fast-food scenario was tendered and accepted as an expert on lost profits. The witness might still expect to undergo something like the following cross-examination:

QUESTION: Your primary consulting work involves business valuation, correct?

QUESTION: Issues of valuation usually involve an existing business, right?

QUESTION: People come to you when they want to buy or sell a business, or when they have to value it for estate tax purposes, or perhaps when there is a divorce?

QUESTION: You wouldn't call yourself a management consultant, would you?

QUESTION: So someone who wanted assistance in expanding a business would need to go to a different consultant, right?

QUESTION: For example, there are consultants who specialize in site evaluation, correct?

QUESTION: But you don't do that, do you?

QUESTION: So if someone wanted to evaluate the best possible locations for business outlets, you would recommend consulting someone else, wouldn't you?

The lawyer will now argue to the court that the crucial issue of location is beyond the witness's expertise and that her opinion regarding lost profits should therefore be disallowed.

b. Stressing Missing Credentials

An expert witness may be qualified to testify, but the cross-examiner may still show that he lacks certain important certifications, degrees, or licenses. Assume, for instance, that the plaintiff in a personal injury action has called his psychotherapist to testify on the issue of damages. The witness was tendered and accepted as an expert and has completed his direct testimony:

QUESTION: Your degree is in social work, correct?

QUESTION: You do not have a doctorate in clinical psychology, do you?

QUESTION: And, of course, you are not a psychiatrist?

QUESTION: I notice that your stationery lists your name as Elliott Middleton, MSW.

QUESTION: I have seen other social workers with the letters ACSW after their names; doesn't that stand for accredited clinical social worker?

QUESTION: That is an additional certification that some social workers earn, correct?

QUESTION: But you have not achieved that certification, have you?

Of course, there is no shame in lacking a particular credential. But that will not prevent a cross-examiner from pointing out its absence, or even using it in an effort to embarrass or diminish the witness.

c. Contrasting Credentials

Missing credentials are most likely to be emphasized when their absence can be contrasted with an opposing expert's "superior" qualifications. In the following example, assume that the plaintiff called a practicing attorney as an expert witness in a legal malpractice case. This scenario is then taken from the defendant's cross-examination:

QUESTION: Mr. Rose, you say on your resume that you are a member of the American Bar Association Section of Litigation, correct?

QUESTION: The American Bar Association Section of Litigation is open to any lawyer who is willing to pay the dues, isn't it?

QUESTION: So you were not elected or chosen by your peers for membership in that section, were you?

QUESTION: I assume you are familiar with the American College of Trial Lawyers?

QUESTION: That organization consists of lawyers who specialize in litigation and the trial of cases, right?

QUESTION: Membership in the American College is limited to two percent of the lawyers in any given state, isn't that right?

QUESTION: And individuals have to be proposed and elected to membership in the American College of Trial Lawyers?

QUESTION: You are not a member of the American College, are you?

QUESTION: But you are aware, aren't you, that the defendant's expert, Ms. Yeats, is a member of the American College of Trial Lawyers?

Experts' credentials may be contrasted on bases other than certification. It is fair to point out an expert's greater or more specific experience, teaching or publication record, or any other disparity that might enhance one witness and diminish the other.

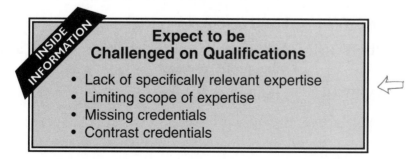

Expect to be Challenged on Qualifications

INSIDE INFORMATION

- Lack of specifically relevant expertise
- Limiting scope of expertise
- Missing credentials
- Contrast credentials

D. Obtaining Favorable Information

Once the issue of qualification has been resolved, most lawyers will begin their cross-examinations by attempting to obtain favorable information from the opposing expert. This segment of the examination is usually cordial and nonconfrontational, as lawyers heed the admonition to "be friendly first."

In a case of any complexity, it is almost certain that the expert will have some information that will be helpful to the cross-examiner's case. Frequently it will fall into one of the following categories.

1. Affirming the Other Expert

Even experts who disagree with each other will usually have many shared understandings. Thus, a witness may be asked to acknowledge the reliability of the opposing expert's data, the validity of her assumptions, or the caliber of her credentials.

2. Eliciting Areas of Agreement

Counsel may also ask an expert for certain concessions on the merits of the case. For example, the cross-examiner may ask the expert to agree with several of his major premises, even though the witness's ultimate conclusion is unfavorable to the lawyer's case. Consider this cross-examination of the defendant's expert in the drive-in restaurant case:

QUESTION: Dr. Isaacs, you are dissatisfied with the nature of Dr. Lipton's study of lost profits, correct?

ANSWER: Yes, I have trouble with Dr. Lipton's methodology.

QUESTION: But you agree, don't you, that the chain had been operating as a going concern?

ANSWER: Yes, I do.

QUESTION: In fact, the restaurant chain had made a profit every year they were in business?

ANSWER: I believe that is correct.

QUESTION: And every one of their outlets showed at least some profit, correct?

ANSWER: I think that is right.

QUESTION: So someone must have been able to select profitable locations, right?

ANSWER: I suppose so.

QUESTION: Dr. Lipton assumed that the chain would continue to choose good locations, isn't that right?

ANSWER: That is implicit in her model.

QUESTION: And you did not conduct an independent study of favorable or unfavorable restaurant locations, did you?

ANSWER: No, I did not.

QUESTION: So you have no specific data you can point to that would contradict Dr. Lipton's assumption?

ANSWER: I do not.

3. Criticizing Conduct

Although the expert was retained by one party to the litigation, she nonetheless may not approve of all of that party's conduct. Recognizing this, the cross-examiner may ask the witness for specific criticism. In the example below, the plaintiff's expert honestly acknowledges the shortcomings in the plaintiff's own record keeping:

QUESTION: Dr. Lipton, in order for you to reach your opinion on damages it was necessary for you to review all of the plaintiff's financial records, correct?

ANSWER: Yes, that is correct.

QUESTION: Isn't it true that the plaintiff company did not keep accurate store-by-store records?

ANSWER: Yes, they aggregated their financial information, rather than breaking it down store-by-store.

QUESTION: Didn't the absence of store-by-store information make your job much more difficult?

ANSWER: I found that I was able to achieve accurate results on the basis of statewide projections.

QUESTION: I understand your position. Still, you could have projected profits for each individual restaurant if the available financial data had been more precise, isn't that true?

ANSWER: That is true.

QUESTION: But because of the plaintiff's aggregate records, you were not able to do that?

ANSWER: No one could have made such projections on the basis of those records.

Note that at one point the cross-examiner asked the witness to agree with a characterization—the absence of store-by-store information made the job "much harder." The witness replied by explaining how she was still able to achieve accurate results. The lawyer then reverted to more factual questions and the witness responded by continuing her criticism of the plaintiff's records.

E. Learned Treatises

One form of cross-examination unique to expert witnesses is the use of a "learned treatise." Under the Federal Rules of Evidence, an expert witness may be confronted with statements contained in "published treatises, periodicals, or pamphlets on a subject of history, medicine, or other science or art," so long as the source is established as a reliable authority.[2]

The witness will often be asked whether she relied on a particular treatise in reaching her opinion or, failing that, whether she acknowledges it as authoritative in the field. Such questions are a sure tip-off that the attorney is about to read a passage from the book that contradicts (or seems to contradict) the witness's testimony.

Note, however, that the witness may be cross-examined concerning the treatise whether or not she has relied on it and even if she does not acknowledge it as authoritative. Under the Federal Rules of Evidence, the reliability of a learned treatise may be established either by admission of the witness, or by other expert testimony, or even by the court's own "judicial notice."[3] The cross-examination, then, could conceivably take this form:

QUESTION: Are you familiar with Steven Lubet's *Modern Trial Advocacy*?

ANSWER: Certainly.

QUESTION: Do you regard that treatise as authoritative in the field?

---

2. Rule 803(18), Federal Rules of Evidence. The practice is similar in most state jurisdictions.
3. Rule 803(18), Federal Rules of Evidence.

ANSWER: Absolutely not.

QUESTION: I want to read you a passage from Lubet's *Modern Trial Advocacy*.

OPPONENT: Objection, Your Honor. The witness testified that Lubet is not regarded as an authority.

QUESTION: Your Honor, we will produce other expert testimony that Lubet's treatise is regarded as an authoritative text.

COURT: You may proceed.

Once the reliability of the treatise has been confirmed, the cross-examination may proceed in either of two ways. The lawyer may simply read a passage from the treatise into evidence without asking the expert any questions about it; the Federal Rules require only that the excerpt be called to the witness's attention.

The more traditional approach is to ask the witness whether she agrees with the particular quotation. At that point the expert may either accede or disagree. Of course, the witness might well want to explain any disagreement, but she may or may not be able to do that during cross-examination.

F. Impeachment

Impeachment is intended to discredit the witness as a reliable source of information. Successful impeachment renders the witness less worthy of belief, as opposed to merely mistaken or unobservant. The most common method of impeaching expert witnesses is the use of a prior inconsistent statement. The elicitation of a prior inconsistency demonstrates that the witness's current testimony is at odds with her own previous statements. In essence, such an examination says, "Do not believe this witness because her story has changed."

It is easy to see the potential for drama in confronting a witness with a prior inconsistent statement. Indeed, it is the moment that cross-examiners live for—the opportunity to show that the witness's current testimony is contradicted by her own earlier words. Prior inconsistent statements damage a witness's credibility because they demonstrate that the witness has altered her account. Depending upon the nature and seriousness of the change, and the presence or absence of an explanation, the witness may be shown to be evasive, opportunistic, error-prone, or even lying.

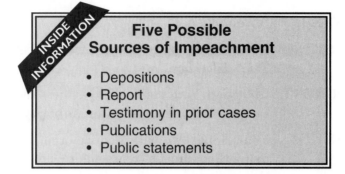

Regarding experts, prior inconsistencies may be drawn from depositions, testimony in previous cases, publications, or any other source for the witness's own earlier pronouncements. Whatever the origin of the witness's words, there is basically a single format for impeachment. The lawyer will (1) recommit the witness to his current testimony, (2) validate the prior statement, and (3) confront the witness with the inconsistency.

The following illustration, though somewhat truncated, places the entire process in perspective.

Recommit:

QUESTION: Doctor, you testified during your direct examination that you observed bruises of varying ages, correct?

ANSWER: That is right.

Validate:

QUESTION: You made notes on the patient's medical chart immediately after you examined him, didn't you?

ANSWER: I did.

QUESTION: You understood that it was important for your notes to be accurate, didn't you?

ANSWER: Yes.

QUESTION: And you made those notes on the very day of the examination, right?

Confront:

QUESTION: Please look at Exhibit Number 25 and tell me if you recognize your handwriting.

ANSWER: I do.

QUESTION: Isn't this the medical chart we were just discussing?

ANSWER: It is.

QUESTION: And doesn't your entry on the chart state: "Observed multiple blue-green contusions on the anterior upper extremities"?

In an actual case the impeachment will probably have a longer build-up. The lawyer will have to attend to certain technical requirements, omitted above, and will also probably attempt to milk the situation for some additional drama—perhaps using an enlargement of the report or waving it in the witness's face.

A good lawyer will not ask the witness for an explanation of the inconsistency.

G. Challenging Impartiality

Expert witnesses need to be independent analysts, not advocates in the case. One of the worst accusations that can be made against an expert is that he has altered his opinion to fit a party's needs. Obviously, then, it can be very effective to cross-examine an expert on the issue of bias if the material is there to be exploited. Cross-examination on bias tends to fall into three basic categories.

1. Fees

Most experts in litigation are retained and paid fees. While the acceptance of money in exchange for testimony would initially seem to be a likely area for cross-examination, in reality such cross is not usually pursued.

First, the fact finder will probably understand that no witness could afford to perform extensive tests or analyses without being compensated. Second, all experts in the case are probably being paid, so the lawyers usually have little to gain by making a point of it on any particular cross-examination.

Cross-examination on fees is generally seen only in fairly limited circumstances, such as where the fee is inexplicably large or where the witness has a significant unpaid balance outstanding at the time of testimony.[4]

---

4. Certain fee arrangements are unethical; these are discussed in Chapter Nine, section E.

2. Relationship with Party or Counsel

An expert's relationship with a party or counsel may also be used to imply a lack of impartiality. Some witnesses seem to work repeatedly with certain law firms (or litigants), testifying to similar conclusions in case after case. While such an ongoing relationship is not proof of actual bias, cross-examiners can be counted on to insinuate that the association must have been sustained for a reason.

Some cases may involve testimony by in-house experts, perhaps a company's own accountant or engineer. In most cases, such experts are susceptible to no more suggestion of bias than could be any other employee. In some situations, however, the in-house expert's own judgment will be at issue in the case. An accountant, for example, may have failed to see that a debt was undercollateralized; an engineer may not have foreseen the need for more exacting tolerances. In these circumstances an expert can expect the cross-examination to dwell on the witness's personal stake in the litigation.

3. Positional Bias

With or without past retention, some experts become closely identified with certain professional, scientific, or intellectual positions. Experts frequently come to testify only for plaintiffs or only for defendants. Others reach only one of a range of conclusions. For example, it is said that some psychiatrists have been known never to find a single criminal defendant to be sane or competent.

In preparing for trial, lawyers will seek out evidence of such real or imagined rigidity, as the suggestion of inflexible "positional bias" can be exploited effectively on cross-examination.

INSIDE INFORMATION

**Expect to be
Cross-Examined on Bias**

- Relationship to counsel
- Relationship to client
- Preconceptions and professional attitudes
- Fees

H. Omissions

An expert may be vulnerable on cross-examination if she has failed to conduct essential tests or procedures, or if she has neglected to consider all significant factors. Virtually every expert should anticipate some cross-examination along this line. No matter how well prepared the witness, basic mathematics tells us that there will be an infinite number of things she did not do. Of course, many of the supposed omissions will be trivial or meaningless, but others may turn out to be significant.

Experts in certain fields are frequently asked to give evaluations concerning the validity or accuracy of other experts' work. A consulting pathologist, for example, might be asked to reevaluate the protocol of an autopsy conducted by the local medical examiner. No matter how prominent, a "second opinion" witness can surely expect to be cross-examined on the fact that he did not conduct the primary investigation.

QUESTION: Dr. Judson, you reach a conclusion quite different from the conclusions reached by Dr. Arlington, correct?

QUESTION: Of course, you did not perform an autopsy yourself, did you?

QUESTION: In fact, your information comes exclusively from Dr. Arlington's autopsy protocol?

QUESTION: So you have relied on Dr. Arlington for all of your factual information, isn't that right?

QUESTION: You know nothing of the actual circumstances of the autopsy, other than what you have learned from Dr. Arlington's report?

QUESTION: So at least with regard to gathering information, you have trusted Dr. Arlington's work?

This technique is not limited to "reevaluating" experts. It may also be directed at any witness who relies exclusively on information provided by others.

QUESTION: Dr. Amiko, you base your opinion solely on an examination of hospital records, correct?

QUESTION: You did not examine the decedent yourself, did you?

QUESTION: So your opinion can only be as good as the information you received, right?

QUESTION: If any of that information were faulty, that could affect the basis for your opinion, correct?

QUESTION: The same would be true of missing information, right?

QUESTION: You'll agree, won't you, that firsthand observation is preferred for the purpose of diagnosis?

Finally, many experts will testify on the basis of statistics or studies compiled from other sources. Frequently, such experts will not have investigated the reliability of the underlying data, and this may leave them vulnerable to cross-examination.

I. Substituting Information

1. Changing Assumptions

Almost all experts must use assumptions of one sort or another in the course of formulating their opinions. An expert's assumptions, however, might be challenged as unrealistic, unreliable, or unreasonably favorable to the retaining party. It is common, therefore, and often effective, for the cross-examiner to ask a witness to alter an assumption—substituting one that is more favorable to the lawyer's own client.

Consider this scenario from the drive-in restaurant case:

QUESTION: Dr. Lipton, your lost-profits calculation includes an assumption that vehicle miles will continue to grow at the rate of 4%, correct?

ANSWER: Yes, that is the figure I used.

QUESTION: Will you agree that numerous factors can influence growth of vehicle miles?

ANSWER: Yes, I think that is obvious.

QUESTION: For example, vehicle miles actually fell during the last recession, didn't they?

ANSWER: I believe that is true.

QUESTION: And if vehicle miles were to rise at a rate of less than 4%, your estimate of lost profits would have to be reduced, correct?

ANSWER: Yes, that is right.

QUESTION: In fact, if we used an assumption of 2%, wouldn't your estimate of lost profits have to be reduced by over $600,000?

ANSWER: I haven't done the calculation, but it should be something in that range.

2. Varying the Facts

A related technique is to vary the facts upon which the expert has relied, or to suggest additional facts, as in this example from the restaurant case:

QUESTION: Dr. Lipton, you are aware that the plaintiff's most profitable outlet was in the Church Station Mall, correct?

QUESTION: And the continued existence of that outlet was a fact that you relied on in calculating your result, right?

QUESTION: But if the entire Church Station Mall were to close due to bankruptcy, then you would have to change your conclusions, right?

QUESTION: Because you couldn't have a profitable restaurant in a closed-down mall, could you?

3. Degree of Certainty

Counsel may also seek to challenge an expert's degree of certainty by suggesting alternative scenarios or explanations:

QUESTION: Dr. Isaacs, you believe that the plaintiff's history of profitability is largely attributable to location, correct?

QUESTION: But there are other factors that contribute to profitability, aren't there?

QUESTION: Some of those factors would be product quality, value, or market demand, right?

QUESTION: And you are surely familiar with the term "destination shopping"?

QUESTION: "Destination shopping" means that people will travel to seek out value or quality or amenities, regardless of location, right?

QUESTION: And you did not interview the plaintiff's customers, did you?

QUESTION: So you cannot be sure that location was of primary importance to them, can you?

QUESTION: Therefore, you cannot rule out the possibility that plaintiff's customers sought out their restaurants because of value or quality?

QUESTION: So you cannot be completely certain that location was the primary factor in the profitability of these particular restaurants?

4. Dependence on Other Testimony

The opinion of an expert often depends upon facts that must be established by other witnesses. Thus, an expert's testimony may be undermined by weakening or attacking its factual underpinnings during the cross-examination of the relevant nonexpert witnesses. Following this method of cross-examination, the lawyer may not even ask the expert about the validity of the subject facts. Instead, the attorney will attempt only to show that the accuracy of some other witness's testimony is essential to the expert's opinion.

QUESTION: Dr. Amiko, part of your opinion is based on Ms. Van Zant's statement that she had never previously been in an accident, correct?

ANSWER: Correct.

Having obtained the crucial admission, counsel may not choose to examine the expert any further on this subject. If Ms. Van Zant's testimony can later be shaken or refuted, the expert's opinion will be weakened as well—a point that the cross-examiner will be sure to point out to the jury during final argument.

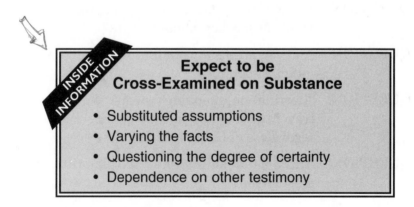

INSIDE INFORMATION

Expect to be Cross-Examined on Substance

• Substituted assumptions
• Varying the facts
• Questioning the degree of certainty
• Dependence on other testimony

— Chapter Seven —

CROSS-EXAMINATION—HOW TO COPE

A. Introduction

Every witness wants to know how to cope with cross-examination. What are the secret techniques for handling the lawyer's questions and resisting the lawyer's craft? In truth, there are few secrets, and no tricks, for dealing with cross-examination. Rather, the primary answer lies in thorough preparation, self-confidence, and steady concentration. A witness will usually survive cross-examination quite well, so long as she has done her work, believes in her position, and listens carefully to the questions.

But surely there must be more to it than that. Certain experts clearly manage cross-examination better than others. Some experts are able to maintain clarity, while others allow their testimony to become muddled or distorted. Some experts remain cheerful, while others become exasperated or visibly riled. What is it that enables individual experts to deal easily with cross-examination, while others are perplexed and frustrated?

As it turns out, there are a number of principles and approaches that can be applied to cross-examination. A witness who has prepared well, and who understands the context of cross-examination, may use these methods to provide answers that are accurate and independent—no matter how tightly the cross-examiner attempts to control the witness's testimony.

B. Redirect Examination

There is one principle that expert witnesses must understand about cross-examination—it is always followed by redirect. Redirect examination is the direct examiner's opportunity to correct any misimpressions created during the cross. Thus, on redirect examination, the expert may be asked to explain any seeming inconsistencies, to add information that the witness was prevented from providing on cross, to fill in any apparent gaps, or to reiterate points that may have been obscured.

It is the retaining lawyer's job, while listening closely to the cross-examination, to decide precisely which issues need to be addressed on redirect. Though gaffes or miscues may seem important to the witness as they occur, they may really be rather trivial in the greater context of the case. Consequently, it is within the lawyer's judgment to determine whether or not particular "problems" need fixing.

This understanding should go a long way toward easing witness anxiety. First, no cross-examination will be perfect; it is expected that even the most experienced witnesses will occasionally answer inartfully or equivocally. Second, redirect provides retaining counsel with ample opportunity to right any wrongs and clear up any ambiguities that might have arisen during cross.

Finally, the expert should be acutely aware that her only responsibility is to answer the questions as they are given. It is not the witness's obligation to solve every problem, provide every explanation, establish every fact, or fill in every gap. That is the lawyer's job. To be sure, a witness will want her answers to be complete and understandable; she will want to expand when necessary and to elaborate when a truncated answer might otherwise be misleading. But the witness does not need to fight for the right to squeeze in every relevant fact and she does not need to argue over the implications of a certain line of questions.

For example, most witnesses on cross-examination find themselves surprised, if not visibly upset, when they are "impeached" with their own prior statements. Invariably, the witness strains to explain why the earlier deposition, report, or article is not actually inconsistent with her current testimony. The witness may well be correct—cross-examinations are often unfair—but the very insistence on arguing may diminish the expert's credibility. Consider this condensed example[1] of witness impeachment:

QUESTION: Dr. Isaacs, you testified today that location is the most important factor in the profitability of a restaurant, correct?

ANSWER: That is my opinion in this case.

---

1. For the sake of brevity, the technical requirements of impeachment have been omitted.

QUESTION: Let me read from an article that you published in *Profits* magazine. Didn't you write: "It is easy to overestimate the importance of location"?

ANSWER: *Yes, but* you are reading it in a misleading way.

QUESTION: Dr. Lipton, didn't I quote you accurately: "It is easy to overestimate the importance of location"?

ANSWER: *Yes, but* you haven't read the whole point.

QUESTION: Let's try again. Doesn't your article say, "It is easy to overestimate the importance of location"?

ANSWER: *Yes, but* that isn't what I meant.

At this point it will be difficult, if not impossible, for the witness to explain why he appears to have written something that he did not mean. The constant stream of "yes, but" answers can only threaten to drown the witness in equivocation.

Now assume that the witness simply agreed that he had written the passage in question, and the cross-examination proceeded to its conclusion. On redirect the witness will be given a full, unapologetic opportunity to explain:

QUESTION: Dr. Isaacs, opposing counsel read a passage from your article in *Profits* magazine. Did he read it to you in context?

ANSWER: No, he read a sentence fragment. He left out most of the paragraph.

QUESTION: What else did you say in that article?

ANSWER: I began that particular section by saying, "It is well understood that location is the single most important factor in a restaurant's profitability, though there are certainly other factors to be considered. Too many restaurateurs think that a good location guarantees success. But no one can succeed without a good product and plenty of hard work." Then I went on to explain that it is easy to "overestimate" the importance of location.

QUESTION: So, to be clear: Is location the single most important factor in profitability?

ANSWER: It certainly is.

QUESTION: Is that what you wrote in your article in *Profits*?

ANSWER: That is exactly what I wrote.

QUESTION: And is that consistent with your testimony today?

ANSWER: The *Profits* article supports my testimony today.

No matter how grueling the cross-examination, a full opportunity to explain every important factor and detail will come soon enough.[2] Redirect examination is a near-universal restorative in which witnesses may take heart.

C. Responding to Cross—General Principles

The following principles may be applied in almost all circumstances.

INSIDE INFORMATION

Nine Principles for Responding to Cross

- Cooperate as much as possible
- Stay calm
- Think before answering
- Understand the question
- Make reasonable "concessions"
- Recognize the legal standard
- Take opposing views seriously
- Read the documents
- Become familiar with the courtroom

---

1. Cooperate as Much as Possible

Until proven otherwise, the cross-examiner is not the witness's personal adversary, much less her enemy. The cross-examiner is entitled to ask questions, even hard questions, and it is the expert's job to answer them as well as possible. A cooperative witness will want to explain her opinion, not defend it inflexibly. Cooperation can be quite disarming and can often defuse even the most tense situations.

---

2. In most courts, the so-called Rule of Completeness provides that once a witness has been impeached on cross-examination, the direct examiner may request the immediate reading of additional, explanatory portions of the same statement. Under the Federal Rules of Evidence, for example, the witness may be allowed to add any other part of the statement or document "which ought in fairness to be considered contemporaneously" with the impeachment. Rule 106, Federal Rules of Evidence.

Needless to say, cooperation should not be confused with passivity. The witness's role is to answer questions accurately, not to be led around by the nose. There is no need to agree with everything the lawyer says or suggests, no matter how positive or intimidating the tone of the question. The witness should not allow herself to be pushed or steered into agreement with false or misleading propositions.

On the other hand, the witness should not disagree merely for the sake of disagreement or to play "gotcha!" with the attorney.

Ultimately, cooperation is simply the right thing to do—unless the attorney makes it impossible.

2. Stay Calm

A calm demeanor is often a witness's best protection against a lawyer's assaults. The cross-examiner is almost always pleased when an expert "loses her cool," since the loss of composure may make the witness seem biased or partisan. It is not unknown for lawyers to attempt to bait or goad witnesses into displaying irritation or anger. While it may seem fair for a witness to shout back at a shouting lawyer, the structure of the trial makes this a decidedly unfair (and unwise) exchange.

First, the lawyer is expected to be a combatant. The lawyer is publicly identified with his client and is therefore "entitled" to show emotion over the facts of the case. An expert witness, however, is a technocrat. Emotion conflicts with dispassion and therefore detracts from credibility.

Moreover, the attorney invariably spends much more time with the judge or jury than does any single witness. Thus, a lawyer who loses his temper can come back the next day, contrite and polite, perhaps even openly apologetic. He has the rest of the trial to make up for any perceived misbehavior (and he has numerous opportunities, both before and after the cross-examination, to demonstrate good conduct). In contrast, most witnesses testify only once, and then for only a fraction of the actual trial time. Thus, it may well be impossible to remedy one bad impression.

Is it ever acceptable for an expert witness to show displeasure while testifying? Of course, witnesses are human and will naturally respond, on some level, to repeated prodding. It is reasonable (and perhaps unavoidable) to show indignation in the face of an unjustified personal attack.

Nonetheless, a witness's watchword should be "composure." The closer the attorney comes to "losing it," the more the witness should strive to remain unperturbed.

3. Think Before Answering

Some cross-examination questions are simple, and some are difficult. Some questions seem straightforward but are actually quite complex. Questions may be challenging, misleading, improper, coercive, unfair, or inscrutable. In each of these situations, and in many others, the witness is best served by listening carefully to the question and thinking before answering.

Unfortunately, many aspects of courtroom procedure discourage contemplation. Many trial courts are perpetually in a hurry, rushing to finish one case in order to begin the next. The very rhythm of cross-examination seems to insist upon rapid-fire answers. And the lawyers often appear to speed the process along—asking staccato questions, hovering over the witness, interrupting if the answer isn't given quickly enough. Put this all together, and it is easy to see that it often requires settled determination to ensure that the witness can take a breath before answering.

In addition, silence can be extremely uncomfortable when sitting on the witness stand. There is a natural tendency, therefore, to fill the silence by speaking, even if the words are coming out more quickly than the thoughts can be assembled behind them.

It would be tempting to say that a witness should take as long as necessary before answering a question, but that would be wrong. In fact, extended silences are indeed barriers to communication, and long, awkward delays can suggest that the witness is uncertain or ill-informed.

Thus, expert witnesses should prepare themselves, through drill if necessary, to pause briefly, but not unnaturally, before answering questions on cross-examination. The reply is probably coming too quickly if the witness answers reflexively; the response may seem too hesitant if the witness takes too long.

Of course, some answers require more than a moment of thought. The cross-examiner may pose a hypothetical that the expert never previously considered. There may be several reasonable alternative responses to a single inquiry. The question may have any number of important implications. All of these situations may require serious reflection, if not outright contemplation, before the witness can answer accurately.

When faced with a truly intricate or challenging question, there is no way to avoid a bit of extended silence—but there is a way to eliminate the awkwardness that often accompanies a significant pause. The witness should simply let everyone know that she is thinking carefully about the answer. This can be done easily by saying something such as, "Let me think about that for a moment." Alternatively, the witness might assume one of several commonly recognized "thinking gestures," perhaps chewing a pencil or furrowing a brow. Witnesses should take care, however, since some gestures—say, scratching the top of one's head—may be misinterpreted as signs of confusion or bafflement.

Ultimately, of course, it is better to take too long while answering correctly than it is to answer carelessly—but with perfect timing.

4. Understand the Question

Most cross-examination questions are straightforward, but some will be vague, convoluted, ambiguous, or worse. A witness should not answer a question unless she is certain that she understands it. The simplest approach is usually to ask for an explanation:

ANSWER: I'm sorry, but I don't understand the question.

Or,

ANSWER: I don't think I follow you, could you please rephrase your question.

Depending on the question, the witness may need to be more specific,

QUESTION: Isn't it true that you never performed a due care audit?

ANSWER: I'm not familiar with the term "due care audit"; we don't use it in my field. Could you please define it?

It is sometimes impossible for the expert and cross-examiner to arrive at a meeting of the minds. The lawyer may continue asking complex question or may insist on using terms that the witness finds ambiguous, imprecise, or professionally meaningless. In these circumstances, the witness may need to provide her own clarification:

ANSWER: I reviewed the entire patient file and I evaluated each of the test results, so I could tell that the defendant complied with professional standards. Is that what you mean by "due care audit"?

A final word: Witnesses should not feign misunderstanding as a way to avoid answering tough questions. That ploy will be transparent and ineffective.

5. Make Reasonable "Concessions"

Cross-examinations often start with a series of questions aimed at drawing "concessions" from the witness. A competent, objective expert will be willing to make concessions so long as they are reasonable and well-stated.

Such questions are typically prefaced with stock phrases, such as:

> QUESTION: Doctor, don't you agree that bruises can be caused in many different ways?

Or,

> QUESTION: You certainly must admit that there were problems with the way the plaintiffs kept their job-site records?

Or,

> QUESTION: Will you concede that you have no firsthand information about the defendant's psychological condition?

Some experts have a tendency to fight concessions, apparently on the theory that it always hurts to give ground to the cross-examiner. In fact, however, the opposite is true. Willingness to concede the obvious is most often taken as a sign of professionalism and objectivity. The witness who resists at every turn only damages her own credibility. (Skilled cross-examiners may sometimes ask for concessions in a tone of voice calculated to seem patronizing or condescending. This strategy is intended to bait the expert into denying a common sense conclusion. The lawyer wants the expert out on limb where she has to defend an irrational position.)

As a subset of concessions, almost every expert will be asked about "omissions"—the things she did not do or did not evaluate in reaching her opinion. Though it may at first seem embarrassing to listen to a long list of supposed oversights, the fact is that there must always be an infinite number of omissions. For example, for every fact the witness did consider, there will necessarily be an unlimited number of facts that the witness did not consider. To be sure, most if not all of the omissions may be irrelevant or trivial, but that will not prevent the attorney from attempting to score points. The attorney's success ratio will be even higher if the witness attempts to equivocate or to make exaggerated claims about the scope or content of her work.

In short, experts should understand that there are two sides to every case. Virtually every expert opinion will have some components that can be used to support the opposing party, and therefore virtually every cross-examination will involve certain concessions. A witness's comfort level, and therefore her confidence, can actually be enhanced when reasonable concessions are readily made.

6. Recognize the Legal Standard

Expert witnesses are often expected to provide opinions that relate to specific legal standards, which may vary from state to state. For example, in some jurisdictions a psychologist might be asked whether a criminal defendant "lacked the capacity to conform his conduct to the requirements of the law." In malpractice cases of all sorts, it is usually necessary to ask something like "whether the defendant exercised the degree of care required of practitioners of comparable skill and experience."

On cross-examination, an expert witness may be called upon to defend her opinion in reference to a defined legal standard. This can pose a difficult problem, since the legal rule may be altogether incongruent with the criteria in the expert's own field. For example, criminal law often asks questions about "sanity," a concept that has no precise technical meaning to psychiatrists and psychologists.

Nonetheless, the law is the law—especially in court—and an expert cannot deny the relevance of a particular legal principle. The refusal to answer a "legal standard" question may render the expert's testimony ineffectual or useless.

The challenge for an expert witness is to provide a professionally competent *and* legally relevant answer. This can usually be done by breaking the question into its constituent facts or components. Imagine a social worker being questioned about a legal concept, such as "due care":

QUESTION: Isn't it true that the defendant always exercised due care in providing psychotherapy to Mr. Thomas?

Given the way the question is phrased, a "yes or no" answer would be inaccurate, and no doubt exploited by the cross-examiner. The witness could probably answer, in all honesty, something like:

> ANSWER: "Due care" is not a concept that has a conclusive meaning in the social work profession.

But, of course, that would undermine the very purpose for which she was called to the stand.

The better approach would be to recognize the legal standard, while explaining the answer in professional terms:

> ANSWER: I think the best answer to your question is that competent social workers would have scheduled more meetings with Mr. Thomas and would have alerted the hospital about a possible suicide attempt.

The witness has not argued with or challenged the legal standard, though she implicitly declined to adopt it as her own. Note, however, that the witness did provide an answer completely responsive to the cross-examiner's question.

7. Take Opposing Views Seriously

In most significant litigation there will be well-qualified experts on both sides. Though opposing experts, by definition, will be in disagreement, there is no need for them to belittle or denigrate each other. A witness's testimony will be taken more seriously when she extends the same courtesy to other witnesses with whom she takes issue.

On cross-examination, a witness who is overtly open-minded will be less susceptible to tough questioning by opposing counsel; and she will be even less vulnerable to ad hominem attacks.

Consider this bit of cross-examination:

> QUESTION: You understand that Dr. Isaacs testified that your analysis is flawed?

> ANSWER: Dr. Isaacs teaches at a second-rate university, and it is doubtful that he will ever get tenure.

One can only begin to imagine the devastating riposte that will follow such an imperious reply. Of course, few witnesses would ever be quite so arrogant, but any personal criticism of the opposing expert (rather than of his views or work) clearly invites retaliation in kind.

To be sure, there is no need to validate another expert's faulty opinion, but the point can be made with a measure of respect:

QUESTION: You understand that Dr. Isaacs testified that your analysis is flawed?

ANSWER: I've read Dr. Isaacs's report, and I do understand that he disagrees with me. I would be pleased to explain the three basic errors in his work-up.

Most trial lawyers agree that it is unwise to attack an expert witness unless the expert has actually done or said something to deserve the assault. An expert's nasty reproach of another witness is exactly the sort of testimony that opens the figurative door to aggressive cross-examination.

8. Read the Documents

Experts are frequently cross-examined regarding the contents of documents. The questions may be as innocuous as whether the witness had an opportunity to review certain files, or they may be as confrontational as impeachment from the expert's own prior writings. Whatever the situation, the witness should take the necessary time to read the document before responding to questions.

There is a technical drill for the use of documents at trial. It usually begins something like this:

QUESTION: Dr. Shiraishi, I am showing you a document that has been marked Defendant's Exhibit 14. Do you recognize it?

The witness will be tempted to glance at the document, perhaps only at its first page, and then respond on the basis of general familiarity.

ANSWER: Yes, I recognize it.

In lawyers' terms, the foundation has now been laid for cross-examining the witness on the document's entire contents.

Problems can arise, however, because many documents may appear superficially similar. Dr. Shiraishi may think that she recognizes a particular medical chart, only to realize several questions down the road that it contains several pages that she has never previously seen. (It is extraordinarily unusual for a lawyer to try to trick a witness into testifying from a substituted document, but it has been known to happen.)

At a minimum, the witness should examine every page of the proffered exhibit. If the document is too long to read thoroughly, the witness should say so before continuing:

121

ANSWER: This patient folder contains about 20 pages. I've just looked through them and they seem in order, but I haven't had time to read everything.

Of course, the witness should not disclaim familiarity with her own records ("it *looks like* my handwriting, but I can't be absolutely sure"), but neither should she assume that the contents of a lengthy file have remained exactly as she last saw them.

In any event, the witness should not limit review of a document to the opening question. She may need to reread it or turn to another page at some other point in the examination.

Part of a admonish on stress reduction for expert witness?

9. Become Familiar with the Courtroom

Cross-examination is inherently uncomfortable, and many attorneys seem to do their best to heighten the witness's discomfort. In response, the witness should take whatever steps might be possible to reduce the stress level.

People tend to work better in familiar surroundings. For most witnesses, however, the courtroom is a decidedly unfamiliar environment. Even experienced witnesses may feel out of place or somewhat ill at ease in a strange courtroom. Consequently, a certain amount of anxiety may be eliminated simply by becoming familiar with the setting in which the expert's testimony will occur.

The witness should make every effort to spend some time in the courtroom before she is called to testify. Explore its dimensions. Check out the sight lines. If possible, get a sense of the acoustics by sitting in the witness stand and speaking to someone in the jury box. If permitted by the local rules of procedure, it may also be helpful to watch other witnesses testify at earlier sessions of the trial.

D. Responding to Cross—Types of Questions and Answers

1. Full Sentences

As we have repeatedly seen, the attorney's goal on cross-examination is to dominate the examination and control the expert's testimony. While the witness will want to teach and explain, the lawyer's objective is ordinarily to restrict the answers as much as possible. In turn, the witness will want to "create some space" in which she can expand upon her answers when necessary.

One simple way to do this is through the use of complete sentences—beginning at the very start of the cross-examination. Rather than answering questions "yes or no," the witness can give an accurate, cooperative response using a full sentence. For example,

QUESTION: You were retained by the attorneys for the defendant, correct?

ANSWER: Yes, I was asked to review the medical records and reach an opinion about the quality of care.

Or,

QUESTION: Your study relied primarily on population growth and vehicle miles, right?

ANSWER: That's right, I used population growth and vehicle miles to determine the expansion of the market.

By using complete sentences in response to initial questions, a witness can begin to establish the right to give full answers throughout the examination. In effect, the witness can set the precedent that responses will not be confined to a single word.

At the outset of the examination the full-sentence answers are used simply as affirmations; later, should the examination become more contentious, the full sentences will be used for explanations. Once that pattern is in place, it is much less likely that the witness will have to fight to be able to explain. (And lawyers who abruptly attempt to restrain the answers will reveal themselves as unfair.)

2. "Yes or No"

Witnesses, especially experts, are under no obligation to answer every question "yes or no." Of course, the witness should be cooperative and should respond to questions in good faith, but some questions just cannot be answered in monosyllables, no matter how strenuously the attorney insists.

QUESTION: You never performed a due care audit, did you?

ANSWER: We do not use that term in my field.

QUESTION: Just answer "yes or no." You never performed a due care audit, did you?

ANSWER: I'm sorry, but the way you have phrased it makes it impossible for me to answer "yes or no."

At this point the attorney has three choices. He can rephrase the question, he can ask the witness for an explanation, or he can drop the subject and go on to another. Whichever path the lawyer follows, the witness has avoided giving a misleading answer.

Note that the witness in the above example did not argue with the lawyer. The witness also offered a reason for her inability to answer without an explanation. Consequently, it is unlikely that a judge would direct her to respond "yes or no." An argumentative witness, however, might draw a reprimand from the court.

3. Predicate Questions

Some questions on cross-examination include an implicit predicate. Any answer to such questions can tend to be misleading, since it may be understood as accepting the assumed fact. The witness, however, does not need to accept the assumptions in the questions.

Consider the following:

QUESTION: Dr. Lipton, in a mature market, isn't it true that location is especially important to a restaurant's profits?

The question contains the implication that the case at trial involves a "mature market." An affirmative answer will suggest that the witness accepts the characterization, whether it is accurate or not. To be sure, the question must be answered, but the witness should clearly identify the nature of the assumption:

ANSWER: I can't agree that we are talking about a mature market. Would you still like me to answer the question?

Or,

ANSWER: Your question assumes a mature market, which I think is inaccurate.

Or,

ANSWER: When there is a mature market, unlike the situation here, I agree that location is particularly important.

4. Explanations First (The "Yes, But" Dilemma)

As we have repeatedly seen, the cross-examiner's objective is to prevent the witness from including any explanation in her answers.

One way for the lawyer to achieve this goal is by cutting off the witness's answer before she reaches the explanation. The lawyer uses just that technique in the following example of impeachment:[3]

QUESTION: You testified today that you observed bruises that varied in color, correct?

ANSWER: I did.

QUESTION: Doesn't your entry on the chart state: "Observed multiple blue-green contusions on the anterior upper extremities"?

ANSWER: Yes, but . . .

QUESTION: Thank you. So the only color mentioned on the chart is blue-green, right?

ANSWER: Yes, but . . .

QUESTION: You have answered the question. Nothing further.

Even when the witness is allowed to continue, the "yes, but" format is inherently weak. It suggests that the witness basically agrees with the attorney, and everything that follows may be regarded as a quibble.

The witness can avoid this problem by reversing the order of her answer:

QUESTION: Doesn't your entry on the chart state: "Observed multiple blue-green contusions on the anterior upper extremities"?

ANSWER: Blue-green bruises do vary in color, so the answer is "yes."

When faced with a question that requires a qualified answer, the witness can avoid the "yes, but" dilemma by giving the explanation before the affirmation.

5. The Unexpected Negative

Unreasonable questions can come in all formats. We have reviewed a few examples in the preceding sections, including the concealed predicate, the "yes or no" demand, and the qualified affirmation. Inventive lawyers will no doubt continue to devise questions that make a witness's life difficult. The common thread among

---

3. The technical formalities have been omitted.

all these questioning formats is that they confine the expert's ability to explain. The questions *seem* to require only an affirmation. Indeed, everyone in the courtroom, including the cross-examiner, expects nothing more than an affirmation.

Perhaps only the witness realizes that a simple "yes" would be inaccurate or misleading. If the cross-examiner is skilled, however, there may be little or no room for the witness to add an explanation. In these situations, the witness may respond with an "unexpected negative."

In the following example, the cross-examiner asks a series of short, tight, propositional questions. The witness is given virtually no opportunity to explain:

QUESTION: Your report lists the factors you considered in reaching your conclusion on lost profits, correct?

ANSWER: Correct.

QUESTION: And you wrote down the important factors, right?

ANSWER: Right.

QUESTION: You listed population growth as a factor, right?

ANSWER: I did.

QUESTION: And that means that you considered population growth, correct?

ANSWER: Yes.

QUESTION: You also listed vehicle miles, didn't you?

ANSWER: Yes, I did.

QUESTION: Meaning that you considered vehicle miles, right?

ANSWER: That is right.

QUESTION: You did not list restaurant location as a factor that you considered, did you?

Everything points to a one-syllable affirmation: the rhythm of the examination, the structure of the questions, the ready agreement in the previous answers. The lawyer expects the witness to say "right," but the witness realizes that an unexplained answer will be misleading or incomplete. Perhaps she will ask for permission to explain,

ANSWER: I would like to explain something about location.

The lawyer will have none of it,

> QUESTION: Just answer "yes or no." Your report did not list restaurant location as a factor, am I right?

Now is the time for the "unexpected negative,"

> ANSWER: In that case, my answer is that you are wrong.

Now the attorney has only two choices. He can accept the witness's answer and proceed with the examination, or he can request an explanation. But note how the natural expectation has shifted; everyone in the courtroom is now waiting for the lawyer to ask the witness to explain. Many lawyers will not be able to resist:

> QUESTION: In what way does your report list location as a factor?

The witness has now been invited to explain.

6. Learned Treatise

An expert witness may be cross-examined concerning any so-called learned treatise that has been recognized by the court as a reliable authority in the expert's field.[4] Following a fairly minimal foundation—including acceptance of the source by an opposing expert—the cross-examiner may confront the witness with any relevant passage from the particular publication. The expert will then be asked whether she agrees or disagrees with the statement in the treatise.

Lawyers often attempt to bolster their cross-examinations by asking the witness whether she acknowledges a particular treatise (or its author) as authoritative in the field. Once a witness testifies that a certain work is authoritative, it will obviously be very difficult for her to disagree with whatever passage the lawyer chooses to read. For example:

> QUESTION: Dr. Gold, do you recognize *Gray's Anatomy* as being an authoritative source in the field of medicine?
>
> ANSWER: Certainly. Every medical student studies from *Gray's Anatomy*.

---

4.   See Chapter Six, section E. Under the Federal Rules of Evidence, the definition includes "published treatises, periodicals, or pamphlets on a subject of history, medicine, or other science or art." Rule 803(18), Federal Rules of Evidence.

QUESTION: I am going to read to you a passage from *Gray's Anatomy*. Please tell me whether you agree with it: "The hipbone's connected to the thighbone." Do you agree with that statement from *Gray's Anatomy*?

There is nothing a witness can do to prevent a lawyer's use of a learned treatise. Even if the witness denies ever having heard of the book, the lawyer may still use it in cross-examination so long as some other expert testifies that it is a valid authority.

A witness can, however, refrain from blanket endorsements of treatises or authors, no matter how well known they may be:

QUESTION: Dr. Kuo, do you recognize *Gray's Anatomy* as being an authoritative source in the field of medicine?

ANSWER: *Gray's Anatomy* is well respected, but in some matters it is rather out-of-date. There are better, more accurate texts available.

The witness may now either agree or disagree with the proffered passage from *Gray's Anatomy*. By avoiding an across-the-board endorsement, he has preserved his ability to take issue with a specific aspect of the book.

E. Responding to Cross—Trick Questions

Every witness worries about "trick questions." Will the lawyer inveigle me into saying something that I do not really mean? Will the attorney maneuver me into a corner? Will my testimony be twisted into its exact opposite? Most such fears are overstated. There are relatively few trick questions in the lawyers' arsenal, and even fewer that cannot be immediately recognized by well-prepared witnesses and attentive jurors. There are some "tricky" questions, however, meaning questions that require particular caution before the witness answers.

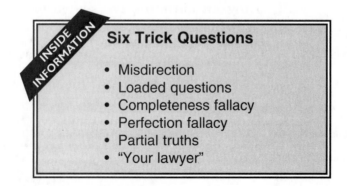

INSIDE INFORMATION

Six Trick Questions

- Misdirection
- Loaded questions
- Completeness fallacy
- Perfection fallacy
- Partial truths
- "Your lawyer"

1. Misdirection and Second-Guessing

Misdirection is a favorite technique of cross-examiners. It is used in the hope that a witness can be baited or enticed into denying the obvious (or even lying), which in turn will detract from the witness's credibility.

A common, though exaggerated, example of misdirection involves the witness's preparation meetings with counsel. Of course, there is absolutely nothing wrong with holding such meetings—no competent attorney would proceed without one—but the cross-examiner hopes that the witness will somehow "feel guilty" about engaging in preparation and will therefore deny it. The lawyer may use a sarcastic tone of voice (indicated in italics below) to enhance the innuendo and further the misdirection:

QUESTION: Dr. Kuo, *you actually met* with the plaintiff's lawyer to *go over your testimony* in this case, *didn't you*?

ANSWER: No, we never went over my testimony.

The witness in this scenario is, at best, hiding the truth. What's more, the plaintiff's attorney, knowing full well that he met with Dr. Kuo several times, will be ethically obliged to make that fact known to the cross-examiner and the court.

To be sure, witnesses should simply never prevaricate, whether lured into it or otherwise. But there is also a deeper lesson. A witness should not attempt to second-guess the cross-examiner's intentions. An expert should be concerned about the meaning of the question and the content of the answer, but it is almost always a mistake to try to figure out what the cross-examiner "is really driving at." That path leads directly into the trap of misdirection.

2. Negative Pregnant—Loaded Questions

Perhaps the only true "trick question" is the negative pregnant—a question to which a denial is actually an admission. The most famous example takes the form "Have you stopped stealing money?" Either possible answer—yes or no—is pregnant with the negative implication that money has been stolen.

An expert witness might conceivably face a negative pregnant question:

QUESTION: Are you still on permanent retainer to the plaintiff's law firm?

The witness will have to answer by disaffirming the question's implied charge:

> ANSWER: I have never been on retainer to any law firm.

There are other forms of loaded questions as well. Their distinguishing feature is the use of imbedded conclusions or characterizations. An expert witness should be alert to questions such as:

> QUESTION: After you lost your original notes, how long did it take you to come up with the new data?

The question above is actually double-barreled. First, it is impossible to answer without accepting the statement that the witness lost his original notes. Somewhat more subtly, it also assumes that the witness "came up" with his data—a negative assertion about the source of the witness's information.

3. The Completeness Fallacy

The completeness fallacy begins by asking the witness to accept a broad overgeneralization. Once given, that agreement can be exploited by the cross-examiner, who will point out that the witness's own work is not in "complete" accord. For example:

> QUESTION: Dr. Lipton, will you agree that profit projections should always be based on a full analysis of every relevant factor?

The statement in the question seems straightforward. Unpacking it, however, we see that it contains several sweeping generalizations: projections should *always* be based on a *full* analysis of *every* relevant factor. A witness who, without qualification, agrees with this statement will soon find herself attempting to defend even the slightest deviation from this unrealistic norm.

> QUESTION: Dr. Lipton, you have agreed that you should always perform a full analysis of every factor, right?

> QUESTION: In projecting lost profits, you did not do a market study of consumer preferences, right?

> QUESTION: You did not evaluate the state's recent application for federal highway funding, did you?

And there will be more. A talented lawyer will be able to identify an unlimited number of ways in which the expert failed to perform a full analysis of every factor. It will not even be that difficult, since no one can *always* perform a *full* analysis of *every* factor. The witness will even have trouble claiming that certain steps were not necessary, since her initial answer acknowledged that one should *always* do everything.

The witness's mistake was answering without qualification. Consider the alternative:

QUESTION: Dr. Lipton, will you agree that profit projections should always be based on a full analysis of every relevant factor?

ANSWER: Profit projections should be based on reliable data and should take the most important and reasonable factors into account.

The lawyer may press the point, rejecting the witness's qualifying explanation:

QUESTION: But my question is, will you agree that profit projections should always be based on a full analysis of every relevant factor? Please answer "yes or no."

In which case the witness might need to engage the unexpected negative:[5]

ANSWER: Given the way you have phrased the question, I will have to answer "no."

The lawyer will now have to choose between asking for an explanation and accepting the witness's answer as given.

4. The Perfection Fallacy

A Latin maxim warns that "best can become the enemy of good," meaning that inflexible insistence on perfection may prevent one from accepting perfectly decent alternatives. In cross-examination, the perfection fallacy seeks to exploit the witness's ideals:

QUESTION: Dr. Kuo, can we agree that it is best to measure blood alcohol levels within one hour after ingestion?

ANSWER: Yes, that is the goal.

QUESTION: But in this case, no blood was taken from the defendant until at least three hours after the accident, right?

---

5. See section D.5, *supra*.

ANSWER: I believe that is right.

QUESTION: Which would be at least four hours after any pos-
            sible ingestion, correct?

ANSWER: Correct.

QUESTION: So it took four times as long as the ideal before
            any blood was taken from the defendant in this
            case.

Of course, what is "ideal" in a laboratory may be impossible in
real life, but the perfection fallacy makes no such allowances. The
witness would be better advised to frame the answer within the context of the case:

QUESTION: Dr. Kuo, can we agree that it is best to measure
            blood alcohol levels within one hour after ingestion?

ANSWER: Blood alcohol can be reliably measured for at
            least six hours following ingestion.

Again, the attorney may press forward:

QUESTION: But isn't it best to do it within one hour?

ANSWER: What is "best" will always depend upon the cir-
            cumstances involved.

5. Partial Truths

Some questions contain partial truths, usually because they are
phrased in a "predicate-conclusion" format. In such questions the predicate may be true and the conclusion false, or vice versa. In either case,
the witness will be tempted to give a "yes, but" answer. We have seen,
however, that "yes, but" responses tend to be misleading or worse.

QUESTION: You had to rely on a technique called "sampling"
            to arrive at your analysis, because the plaintiff's
            financial records were so poor, correct?

In fact, sampling is a reliable tool, whether or not the underlying records have been perfectly kept. But note how poorly a "yes, but" answer will convey this information:

ANSWER: Yes, but we would have used sampling anyhow.

The partial truth has become part of the witness's answer. Now consider an answer that avoids partial truth:

ANSWER: Sampling is a reliable accounting tool that we use in virtually every engagement.

If the lawyer wants to proceed, the question will now have to be uncoupled:

QUESTION: But in this case you used sampling because the records were so poor?

The full truth, however, can now be stated unhindered:

ANSWER: That is wrong. We used sampling because it could give us an accurate result.

The best response to a "partial truth" question is simply to state the whole truth, rather than agree with half of it.

6. Fees

It is reasonable for lawyers to cross-examine experts on the nature of their fee agreements,[6] but sometimes the questions themselves can be unfair and loaded. Here is a typical example of a "partial truth" question on the expert's compensation:

QUESTION: Dr. Gold, isn't it true that you have been paid a fee to come in and testify today that all proper procedures were followed in the surgery that left my client crippled?

While it is true that the witness has been retained for a fee, the question draws an unwarranted connection between payment and the content of the expert's opinion. A simple "yes" answer would validate this innuendo, while a "no" answer would seem evasive or disingenuous. The challenge for the witness is to answer truthfully and accurately:

ANSWER: I am being paid my normal hourly rate for the time I have spent researching this matter and coming into court to answer questions about it.

7. "Your Lawyer"

In order to challenge the independence of an expert, a cross-examiner will often try to show that the witness is closely identified with the retaining client. One way to do this is to refer to

---

6. See Chapter Nine, section E.

the retaining attorney as "your lawyer," suggesting that the expert is virtually a party to the case:

QUESTION: Your lawyer will have an opportunity to ask you questions on redirect examination.

Or,

QUESTION: Now, on direct examination your lawyer brought up the subject of location, didn't he?

It may be fruitless—and it may seem overly defensive—for the expert to argue over definitions on cross-examination. If done at all, it should be done politely:

QUESTION: You met with your lawyer three times before you came in here to testify, correct?

ANSWER: I met with Mr. Burns to review my data, but he is not my lawyer.

Needless to say, the expert should be careful not to pick up on this unfortunate speech pattern:

QUESTION: Dr. Gold, are you familiar with Exhibit 25?

ANSWER: Yes, my lawyer showed it to me several weeks ago.

No matter how good the working relationship between expert and attorney, there is no way that retaining counsel should be considered the expert's lawyer. They are simply two professionals who happen to be working on the same matter.

— Chapter Eight —

DEPOSITIONS AND DISCOVERY

A. Introduction

The term "discovery" refers to the pretrial process by which the parties to litigation obtain information and evidence from each other. Discovery has the noble purpose of attempting to ensure that trials are decided on the merits, rather than by ambush or surprise. Thus, the rules in the federal system, and in nearly every state, provide for broad disclosure of almost everything that might be relevant to the outcome of a case. To be precise, the Federal Rules of Civil Procedure provide that unless a court orders otherwise,

> Parties may obtain discovery regarding any matter, not privileged, which is relevant to the subject matter involved in the pending action. . . . The information sought need not be admissible at the trial if the information sought appears reasonably calculated to lead to the discovery of admissible evidence.[1]

In other words, the parties must give each other access to anything and everything relevant to the case, including books, records, documents, and objects. Additionally, the parties must provide each other with the identities and locations of potential witnesses, who may then be required to give sworn statements prior to trial.[2]

Though the use of discovery was intended to simplify and streamline trials, the involvement of lawyers in the process has—probably inevitably—rendered it burdensome, complex, and

---

1. Rule 26(b)(1), Federal Rules of Civil Procedure.

2. Experts may be divided into two broad categories: those who are expected to testify and those who are not. The identity of testifying experts must be disclosed prior to trial (sometimes called "designating" the expert witnesses), and thereafter they are subject to expansive discovery. Non-testifying experts are those who have been retained only to assist the attorney in preparing or understanding the case. Since they are not expected to testify, their identities do not need to be made known to the opposing parties. In fact, the identities of non-testifying experts (sometimes called "consulting" experts) are often considered confidential. The general rule is that no discovery is available from non-testifying experts except in extraordinary circumstances. Rule 26(b)(3), Federal Rules of Civil Procedure.

prolonged. Discovery in a complicated case may stretch over several years, as the lawyers take countless depositions and wrangle endlessly over the details of production. Numerous reforms have attempted to ease the ordeal, but discovery nonetheless remains the most time-consuming aspect of most litigation.

For most expert witnesses, the three most important aspects of discovery are document production, written interrogatories, and depositions.

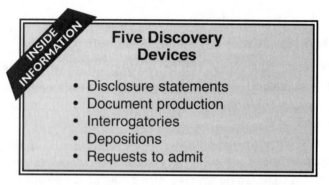

Five Discovery Devices

- Disclosure statements
- Document production
- Interrogatories
- Depositions
- Requests to admit

B. Document Production and Written Interrogatories

1. Document Requests

The most important thing for expert witnesses to know about document production is that it exists. Once an individual has been designated a "testifying expert," she may be required to produce virtually every document she has created, relied upon, reviewed, or possessed in the course of her work on the case. In addition to the more obvious documents in an expert's file—such as correspondence, test results, laboratory reports, photographs, and data compilations—production may also extend to preliminary drafts, work papers, handwritten notes, and personal diaries, so long as they contain information, not privileged, that may be reasonably likely to "lead to the discovery of admissible evidence."

In most jurisdictions, document requests are served upon the attorneys, who then have the obligation of compiling all of the materials necessary for compliance. It is not unusual for a retaining lawyer simply to telephone an expert witness to request something on the order of "your entire file." Although some lawyers may not make it completely clear, it is important for experts to understand that the "entire file" means the entire file. Everything possibly connected to the case should be made available (or at least known) to the retaining lawyer, who will then go through the materials to determine exactly what must be shown to the other side.

Some requested documents may be protected from discovery, including those that are privileged or those that are completely unrelated to the issues in the litigation. But even undiscoverable documents must usually be identified for the opposing parties so that they may pursue the issue with the court. Consequently, doubts about the need to disclose certain materials should be resolved in consultation with the retaining lawyer. The expert should not pre-empt this decision by removing items from her file. The subsequent discovery of undisclosed documents can be embarrassing to the expert and potentially devastating to the client.

In extreme circumstances, the expert may wish to consult her own counsel, rather than depend exclusively on the retaining lawyer. For example, a discovery request might seek documents from one of the witness's prior engagements. The retaining lawyer, with his own client to represent, should not be relied upon to assess the confidentiality of such materials.

Experts may also be called upon to assist in preparing document requests. Many lawyers take a scattergun approach to discovery, asking for items in the broadest and most general possible terms. While catch-all requests are all well and good, specificity is always better since it leaves less room for interpretation or argument.

That is where the expert comes in. In any given case, a lawyer may have a general idea about the nature of the documents that might or might not exist. An expert, however, should have a much more definite understanding about the format, composition, and retention of records and other materials. Consequently, the expert may be called upon to help the retaining lawyer draft document requests so as to make sure that no relevant document goes unrequested.

2. Interrogatories

Interrogatories are written questions that must be answered under oath prior to trial. Though technically directed to the parties themselves, interrogatories are used in many jurisdictions to obtain information about expert witnesses and their expected testimony. While the expert will not usually sign the interrogatory answers herself, she may be called upon to provide the necessary information or even to draft the response.

In one state, for example, interrogatories can require a party to provide the following information regarding every expert witness: (1) the subject matter upon which the expert is expected to testify; (2) the conclusions and opinions of the expert and the bases therefor; and (3) the qualifications of the expert.[3] Other states are more or less expansive, but in each case it is obvious that the expert will have to assist counsel in writing the answers to the relevant questions. In many jurisdictions an expert may submit a written report in lieu of answering interrogatories.

As with document requests, experts may also be called upon to assist in drafting interrogatories. Indeed, it is often vitally important that the expert have some input into the questions that are posed to the opposing side. For example, it is often the case that an expert's opinion will be fact dependent, in that it must be based on a demonstrated or agreed set of circumstances. Interrogatories are the perfect device for establishing such facts, but only if the expert has been able to provide the lawyer with the necessary questions. In the same fashion, an expert may suggest interrogatory questions that might have the effect of undercutting the opposing expert's testimony.

C. Discovery Depositions—Technical Details

A deposition is a sworn statement given before trial for the purpose of giving all parties access to the witness's testimony.[4] Expert depositions are usually taken by the opposing attorney, typically after the expert has completed all of her preparatory work and often (though not always) relatively shortly before the trial date. Because the great majority of lawsuits are settled before trial, the deposition is frequently the only testimony an expert will give in the case.

1. Convening the Deposition

Expert depositions are often arranged by agreement among the attorneys. Either by telephone or letter, the lawyers and the witness are usually able to arrive at a mutually agreeable time and place. Should agreement fail, there are a variety of methods available to require a deposition, including a formal "notice of deposition," subpoena, or court order. The failure to appear for a deposition can result in a number of sanctions against the responsible party, ranging from monetary penalties to exclusion of the witness's testimony.

There is no general requirement that an expert bring her file (or anything else) to the deposition. However, counsel may agree that the

---

3. Rule 213(g), Illinois Supreme Court Rules.

4. A less frequently used format is the "evidence deposition," taken to preserve the testimony of a witness who may not be available at the time of trial. See section H, *infra*.

witness will bring certain items with her, or she may be served with a "subpoena duces tecum" specifying the documents, records, or objects that must be produced at the deposition.

The party taking the deposition has the option of specifying its location—usually the office of the deposing lawyer. In cases where the witness and lawyers do not live in the same city, a room for the deposition may be arranged at a hotel, conference center, or in borrowed space at a local law office. Some courthouses also have deposition rooms available.

Virtually all depositions are recorded by a stenographer. Increasingly, they are recorded by sound and video as well. Most jurisdictions specify that the means of recording must be designated ahead of time, so that the witness will not be surprised by the presence of a video camera.

2. Persons Present

While depositions are official litigation proceedings, they nearly always take place outside of court. Though the questioning is similar to that which occurs at trial, no judge is present to oversee the testimony.[5] In the absence of a judge, the atmosphere at a deposition is usually rather informal, if not exactly relaxed.

An expert's deposition will usually be attended by at least one lawyer for every party in the case. The client's themselves are also entitled to be present, though that is fairly unusual. In some cases, opposing counsel will bring their own experts to watch the deposition, either to assist them in framing questions or to provide an early opportunity to review the testimony.

In addition, every deposition must be attended by at least one person "authorized to administer oaths,"[6] typically the court reporter who will be recording the deposition.

Depending upon the size and complexity of the case, there may be as few as four people in the deposition room, or as many as ten or more.

3. Sequence of Questioning

The deposition begins when the court reporter places the witness under oath. The lawyer who convened the deposition has the first

---

5. In extraordinarily contentious circumstances, a judge may order that a deposition occur in court or in the presence of a specially appointed master or other judicial officer.

6. Rule 28(a), Federal Rules of Civil Procedure.

opportunity to question the witness, followed by every other attorney in attendance. Because there is no judge, the order of questioning may be rather informal, with lawyers interrupting each other and proceeding out of turn.

There is no restriction on the number of times a lawyer may question the witness at a single deposition, though some jurisdictions have time limits.

The retaining lawyer has the last opportunity to ask questions of the expert. In most cases, of course, the retaining lawyer will already know everything the witness has to say, and will therefore have few, if any, questions. Counsel may, however, want to use this occasion to clarify certain issues or clear up any ambiguities.

4. After the Deposition

At the end of the deposition, the witness will be asked whether she wishes to review the transcript in order to correct any possible errors. The offer is often made in shorthand, asking whether the witness "waives or reserves signature." If signature is waived, the transcript, as written by the court reporter, will stand as the official record of the deposition.

If signature is reserved, the witness will be notified when the transcript has been completed and will then have a fixed period—30 days in federal cases—to review it and to make any changes "in form or substance."[7] Many experts prefer to reserve signature, although retaining counsel may have reasons for requesting otherwise.

Upon reviewing a transcript, most changes are fairly mundane, consisting by and large of correcting misspellings and typographical errors. Some changes, however, may be important. The transcription may be garbled or words may be transposed; it is not unknown for a court reporter to have missed or dropped an important word—such as "not"—which can completely change the meaning of the witness's testimony.

In most jurisdictions the witness may go so far as to correct mistakes in her actual testimony, changing or clarifying erroneous answers. Obviously, such changes should not be made lightly. Under the federal rules, the witness must accompany any corrections with "the reasons given by the deponent for making them."[8] Moreover,

---

7. Rule 30(e), Federal Rules of Civil Procedure.
8. Rule 30(e), Federal Rules of Civil Procedure.

substantive changes can become the occasion for embarrassing cross-examination at trial or at a reconvened deposition.

Note that review and signing can be requested by any party, even if the witness herself waives signature.

D. Discovery Depositions—Lawyers' Goals

Lawyers take depositions for six basic reasons: (1) to gather information, (2) to limit the scope of the witness's future testimony, (3) to test or confirm litigation theories, (4) to develop the record for technical legal reasons, (5) to evaluate the witness's credibility and persuasiveness, and (6) to move the case toward settlement.

The following sections discuss these six aims of deposition practice along with the types of questions usually used to pursue each one. Witnesses should understand that deposition goals are complementary and overlapping. In the course of any particular deposition—indeed, in any individual question—an attorney may seek to accomplish as few as one or as many as all six of the possible objectives.

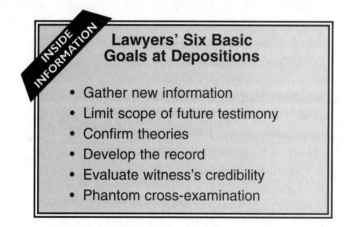

INSIDE INFORMATION

Lawyers' Six Basic Goals at Depositions

- Gather new information
- Limit scope of future testimony
- Confirm theories
- Develop the record
- Evaluate witness's credibility
- Phantom cross-examination

1. Information Gathering

First and foremost, depositions are taken so that the attorney can learn what the witness knows. A good lawyer begins from the premise that the witness has valuable information that needs to be explored and uncovered. In that sense, the lawyer is much like a prospector—searching, probing, and then digging in the most promising areas.

a. Witness Cooperation

The deposing lawyer is not interested in the information simply as a matter of abstract curiosity. He wants to put it to use, preferably in a way that will help him win the case. For that reason, retaining counsel will usually admonish her expert to make deposition answers as short as is honestly possible, so as to minimize the amount of information conveyed. One leading handbook for lawyers recommends that deponents be advised to give short, even one-word, answers:

> If [the questioner] wants more information he will ask for it. The main reason that short answers are best is that attorneys are trained to chase down any paths that appear, just in case there is something relevant at the end. We don't have any desire to prolong this deposition unnecessarily, so it helps everybody if we keep the answers short and to the point.[9]

Many lawyers go further, instructing their experts to expand or explain as little as possible and to make opposing counsel "work for everything he gets."

Notwithstanding that common admonition, it is the witness's duty to be accurate and cooperative, as well as truthful, and to answer deposition questions in good faith. The witness should not regard the deposition as a treasure hunt in which her objective is to foil the lawyer's search. The witness should not conceal information that has reasonably been requested

b. Questioning Technique

Lawyers pursuing information often utilize a questioning style known as the funnel technique. The approach got its name because its format resembles a funnel—wide open at first and narrowing as it proceeds

The initial questions in the funnel sequence will typically invite the witness to share her knowledge:

QUESTION: In your opinion, where did the fire originate?

Or,

QUESTION: Why do you think that the prescribed therapies were ineffective?

Or,

QUESTION: What causes metal fatigue?

---

9. David Malone and Peter Hoffman, *The Effective Deposition: Techniques and Strategies That Work*, 2d ed. (NITA, 1996), 163.

The purpose of these questions is to have the witness begin talking in her own words. The lawyer will probably try to keep this process going as long as possible, using open questions until the subject is exhausted. For example:

QUESTION: What causes metal fatigue?

QUESTION: Are there any other possible causes?

QUESTION: Apart from what you have already told us, might anything else cause metal fatigue?

Variations on the question will continue until the witness says something like:

ANSWER: That's everything. We've covered it all.

The next phase of the funnel method involves tighter, more pointed questions. The lawyer's goal here is to explore some of the topics raised by the first round of answers or to fill in details that the witness may have omitted. Note that the focus remains on gathering information.

QUESTION: Which tests did you run to determine whether metal fatigue was the cause of the product failure?

Or,

QUESTION: Who accompanied you when you investigated the fire scene?

Or,

QUESTION: Please tell us all of the therapies that should have been considered.

At the end of the funnel, the lawyer will recap the line of questioning, closing off the important points by using fully leading questions. The conclusion of the technique is sometimes preceded by an introductions such as, "Let me make sure that I've got this right:"

QUESTION: You spent three hours investigating the fire scene, correct?

QUESTION: You conducted the investigation entirely by yourself, right?

QUESTION: Your conclusions about the place of origin are based on your personal observations, is that right?

Once the funnel is completed, the lawyer can be relatively satisfied that he has learned everything that the witness knows about the particular subject. The deposition may then move on to a new topic.

c. Responses

When properly conducted, the funnel technique is virtually irresistible. It is irresistible because it is sincere. The lawyer truly wants the information and will simply keep asking question until it has all been provided. The best lawyers use an inquisitive, conversational tone, very much the way that a bright student will ask questions of a respected teacher.

2. Limiting Future Testimony

The lawyer's second purpose when taking a deposition is to pin down, and therefore circumscribe, the witness's future testimony.

a. Topic Exhaustion

There is no absolute distinction between information gathering and limiting testimony, since the very act of exhausting a topic also serves to limit what the expert can say about it at trial. That is why the funnel technique concludes by closing off each line of questioning:

QUESTION: Apart from what you have already told us, might anything else cause metal fatigue?

ANSWER: That's everything. We've covered it all.

The expert's trial testimony has now been effectively confined to those matters covered during the deposition.

b. "Freezing" Testimony

There is also a second, more proactive, approach to limiting a witness's future testimony. A lawyer will often come into a deposition with a fairly good idea of an expert witness's likely testimony, especially where the expert has supplied a report or other documentation. In these circumstances, the lawyer may decide to structure the deposition (or part of it) in such a way as to "freeze" the testimony so that the expert cannot expand on it in the future. This tactic relies almost exclusively on short, controlling, leading questions. Consider an example from the fast-food case discussed in earlier chapters:

QUESTION: Dr. Lipton, you based your profit projections on an analysis of population growth and vehicle miles, correct?

QUESTION: You believe that you can obtain an accurate profit projection by estimating growth in population along with increases in miles driven, right?

QUESTION: Your analysis is based on the assumption that statewide figures can give you a reliable forecast for a statewide restaurant chain, correct?

QUESTION: So you did not break the figures down by county, city, or any smaller unit, did you?

QUESTION: You did not conduct a separate analysis of each of the plaintiff's restaurant locations, did you?

QUESTION: The location of the various restaurants was not specifically considered in your calculations, was it?

Note that the lawyer has not even attempted to obtain any new information. Rather, the goal of this deposition was to establish the outer boundary of the witness's work, so that the expert cannot make any new claims at trial about the nature and extent of her analysis.

c. Pinning Down Testimony

Lawyers hate surprises, especially at trial. Therefore, depositions are also used to pin down all of a witness's possible testimony, even if it is damaging to the lawyer's client. That way, at least the testimony will not get worse. Imagine that the lawyer in the following scenario represents the defendant driver in an automobile accident case; the witness is a physician:

QUESTION: Doctor, your report states that you think my client's reflexes were impaired, even though his blood alcohol level was under the legal limit, correct?

QUESTION: Exactly how would his reflexes have been impaired?

QUESTION: What effect would that have on his ability to drive?

QUESTION: Do you think that the impairment would have been noticeable to my client at the time?

Each of the above questions introduces a new set of "bad facts" for the defendant. Nonetheless, the defendant's lawyer will not only ask them, but will pursue them all the way to the end:

QUESTION: What is the basis for your opinion that my client's reflexes would have been impaired?

QUESTION: Would the alcohol have affected his ability to steer?

QUESTION: Would the alcohol have affected his ability to brake?

QUESTION: Would the alcohol have affected his ability to keep a proper lookout?

QUESTION: What leads you to those conclusions?

The lawyer in this situation will no doubt also employ the technique of exhaustion:

QUESTION: Have you explained all of the negative effects on my client's ability to drive safely?

Though it may seem that such negative information will be harmful to the attorney's client, ignorance of the expert's complete opinion would be even more damaging.

d. Responses

It is completely fair for a lawyer to attempt to tie down or confine an expert's testimony. On the other hand, at the time of deposition the witness may not completely understand the full implications of the lawyer's questions. Moreover, it is always possible that the expert will conduct additional research or that new data may come to light.

It is usually prudent, therefore, to avoid giving categorical answers to sweeping questions. A qualified answer will be equally truthful and, in fact, probably more accurate. Consider:

QUESTION: Have you explained all of the negative effects on my client's ability to drive safely?

ANSWER: I believe that I have explained the major effects. There may be others that do not come immediately to mind.

Or,

QUESTION: Apart from what you have already told us, might anything else cause metal fatigue?

ANSWER: Metal fatigue can result from a nearly unlimited number of causes, but I think I have given you the primary factors.

3. Theory Testing

Theory testing is a relatively sophisticated use of the deposition process. In brief, lawyers usually explore several alternative theories in the process of preparing a case for trial. The deposition provides counsel with an opportunity to "test" the various theories to see how well they work. In an expert deposition, the lawyer might pose a series of fairly intricate hypotheticals to the witness in order to determine which ones seem the most promising for development at trial.

In the fast-food case, recall that the plaintiff's expert based her damage projection on estimates of future population growth and increases in vehicle miles. The defendant's lawyer would probably want to try out at least two different theories when deposing the plaintiff's expert. Here is an example:

QUESTION: Dr. Lipton, I would like you to make the following assumptions. First, assume that over half of the plaintiff's restaurants are situated in neighborhoods where growth has been stagnant. Next, assume that over 30% of the plaintiff's restaurants are located a mile or more away from the nearest major traffic artery. Finally, assume that the next three years will see a shortfall in state road funds. Assuming those three things, how would your opinion in this case be affected?

E.g.

The lawyer's theory is fairly obvious—damage projections are "location sensitive." Depending upon the witness's answer, counsel will either pursue it by developing the necessary facts through other witnesses, or he will abandon it as unpromising. And if the first theory doesn't seem to work, there will always be another.

4. Developing the Record

In the course of pretrial litigation, lawyers often need to provide sworn statements in support of various motions and requests to the court. Friendly witnesses are usually willing to sign affidavits when needed, but opposing witnesses may often be less than cooperative. In the case of opposing experts, the necessary sworn statements are typically available only via deposition. Thus, lawyers frequently use depositions to obtain snippets of testimony that they may need for strictly legal-technical reasons unrelated to the expert's actual work.

For example, the date on which an expert was first contacted might be relevant to a "statute of limitations" issue. Similarly, the expert's presence at a client meeting might have some bearing on the assertion of the attorney-client privilege.

5. Evaluating the Witness

The face-to-face encounter at a deposition allows an attorney to size up the witness. Is the expert calm, professional, dignified, thorough, and persuasive? Or is the witness hot tempered, slovenly, erratic, and easily distracted? The answers to these questions may determine the lawyer's eventual approach to cross-examination.

6. Facilitating Settlement

In cases where expert testimony is crucial, an appraisal of the witnesses' deposition performance will almost certainly influence the parties' settlement positions. A lawyer who succeeds in rattling a deponent is likely to become, consciously or unconsciously, much more demanding in settlement discussions. On the other hand, an impressive witness will probably have the opposite effect.

For this reason, many lawyers consciously use depositions as settlement tools. The deposing lawyer may be eager to test the witness's mettle by engaging in what has become known as "phantom cross-examination." Phantom cross-examination is conducted in recognition of the fact that less than 10% of all cases actually proceed to trial. Consequently, in at least 90% of all cases, the expert witness will never be cross-examined in front of a judge or jury. A lawyer who wants to damage an expert's credibility (or attempt to) will probably have to do it at deposition if he harbors any hope that his devastating cross-examination will actually affect the outcome of the case. If the expert's opinion can be undermined or impaired, so the thinking goes, the other side will have to be more forthcoming in the next negotiation.

The flip side of the settlement coin is that the retaining lawyer may well want to "show off" his expert. Rather than tell the expert to be tight lipped and terse, a lawyer who is confident in the settlement potential of his case may well ask the expert to "educate" opposing counsel. Attorneys who take this approach hope that the effectiveness and credibility of the expert's testimony will move the case quickly to a favorable resolution.

E. Discovery Depositions—What to Expect

Discovery depositions are in many ways unpredictable. Given the multiple goals and uses of depositions, there are probably almost as many approaches as there are lawyers and witnesses. Some attorneys are slow and methodical. Others live and die by the short-sharp-shock technique, immediately confronting the deponent with the most inflammatory issues in the case. Nonetheless, there are some areas of question that are almost always pursued in an expert deposition.

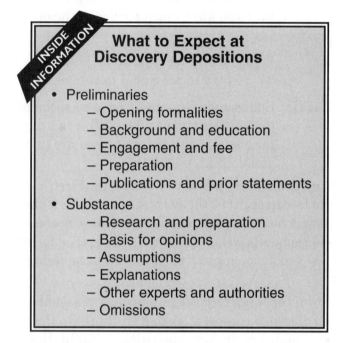

INSIDE INFORMATION

What to Expect at Discovery Depositions

- Preliminaries
  - Opening formalities
  - Background and education
  - Engagement and fee
  - Preparation
  - Publications and prior statements
- Substance
  - Research and preparation
  - Basis for opinions
  - Assumptions
  - Explanations
  - Other experts and authorities
  - Omissions

1. Preliminaries

Many areas of questioning are not directed specifically at the expert's substantive work, but rather at the witness's background, ability to testify, preparation, and the like. Although they will not all necessarily come at the beginning of the deposition, they are still "preliminary" in the sense that they tend to deal with matters that precede the actual development of the opinion.

a. Opening Formalities

Depositions typically begin with a series of formalities. The witness is sworn and the deposing lawyer makes a brief statement for the record identifying the deponent and the other lawyers and parties in attendance.

The next step is usually a "warm-up" phase during which the lawyer explains the format and rules of the deposition, asking the witness to confirm her understanding of the process. Many lawyers use a rather standard series of questions designed to obtain the witness's commitment to providing full and complete answers:

QUESTION: If I ever ask a question that you don't understand, will you please be sure to tell me so that I can re-phrase it?

QUESTION: Will you please tell me if you ever need to clarify or expand on an answer, even if it is an answer that you gave much earlier in the deposition?

QUESTION: If you think that looking at a document might help you answer a question, just let me know and we will try to provide it to you, okay?

QUESTION: Sometimes you might have to speculate or even guess at an answer. That's fine in a deposition, so long as you tell me when you are guessing. Can you do that, please?

Questions of this sort serve two purposes. First, most lawyers truly want to be certain that the witness understands the questions and that there is no confusion about her answers. Second, the series of advance agreements will make it difficult at trial for the witness to explain away an inconvenient or inconsistent answer given at the deposition.

The lawyer's opening requests are usually reasonable, since it is the witness's duty to be cooperative and truthful. On the other hand, blanket agreements are, in fact, impossible to fulfill. How can a witness know whether or not she actually understands a question, especially since her answer may be subject to multiple interpretations in the hands of the attorneys? Thus, a bit of qualification can make the witness's assent more realistic:

QUESTION: If I ever ask a question that you don't understand, will you please be sure to tell me so that I can re-phrase it?

ANSWER: I will certainly tell you if I realize at the time that I don't understand a question.

QUESTION: Will you please tell me if you ever need to clarify or expand on an answer, even if it is an answer that you gave much earlier in the deposition?

ANSWER: I'll do my best.

Many lawyers also make it a practice of asking whether the witness has recently taken any drugs or medications that might interfere with giving accurate testimony. Though it might seem intrusive, the question is not really meant to pry. In the rare case where the witness actually has taken a medication such as a sedative, it is far better to find out at the beginning of the deposition, rather than having to go through the entire process again at a later date.

b. Background and Education

Most expert depositions move fairly quickly into a rather thorough exploration of the witness's background, including education, training, employment history, publication record, and similar information. The questioning may be strictly chronological, or it may be tied in to the subject matter of the case:

QUESTION: Did you take any courses in graduate school that are relevant to your opinion concerning lost profits?

Or,

QUESTION: Have you published any books or articles that cover the subject of metal fatigue?

c. Engagement and Fee

An expert will also usually be asked about the way she came to be engaged in the particular lawsuit. When was she first contacted about the case? Has she ever previously worked on a matter with retaining counsel? What are the terms of the current engagement? How is her fee structured?

Experts should be aware that their conversations and correspondence with retaining counsel are usually subject to full discovery. If, for example, the expert was first contacted by telephone, she can expect several lines of questioning like this:

QUESTION: What did the lawyer tell you about the case during the initial telephone conversation?

QUESTION: Did the lawyer outline any facts or legal theories for you when you first spoke?

QUESTION: What questions did you ask during that first telephone call?

QUESTION: Did you give the lawyer a preliminary opinion over the telephone?

QUESTION: Did you express any doubts or reservations?

Depositions also routinely cover the expert's fee. What is the fee arrangement? How much has been billed so far? Are any invoices outstanding? And, of course, there is always the famous trick question:

QUESTION: What is the fee you are charging for testifying today that all proper procedures were followed in my client's surgery?

ANSWER: I am being paid my normal hourly rate for the time I have spent researching this matter and coming to this deposition to answer your questions about it.

d. Preparation

Another set of questions will cover the witness's preparation for the deposition. In addition to general questions about methods of preparation, the witness will likely be asked to give the details of any preparatory meetings or conversations with retaining counsel. The next question will probably be,

QUESTION: Did you review any documents to refresh your recollection before testifying today?

If the answer is affirmative, the expert (or lawyer) will be asked to produce the relevant documents, as is required by the rules of procedure in most jurisdictions.

e. Publications and Prior Statements

Prior to the deposition, a well-prepared lawyer will have read every relevant book or article ever written by the expert. In addition, the attorney may have tracked down the witness's prior deposition or trial testimony in other cases. An expert witness should therefore be ready to explain or interpret virtually anything she has ever previously said or written on the subjects at issue in the case.

2. Substance

The content of the expert's opinion will ordinarily consume most of the deposition time. The lawyer will want to know everything the expert did, everything she thinks, and every detail and nuance of her opinion. Of course, the nature of the expert's work will vary with the field of specialization, so there is no way to predict the precise scope of the lawyer's questions. There are, however, a number of substantive components that will likely be covered in most depositions.

a. Research and Preparation

At some point in the deposition the expert will be asked to specify all of the steps that she took in researching or preparing her opinion. How did she learn the facts of the case? What authorities did she consult? What tests did she perform? What analyses did she undertake? Whom did she consult?

For each stage or aspect of the witness's preparation, counsel may also ask why or how that particular step supports the expert's ultimate conclusion.

b. Opinions

The expert will be asked to state all of her opinions regarding the issues in the case. If the expert responds with broad conclusions, the lawyer will no doubt ask that they be broken down into more discrete opinions. For example,

QUESTION: What opinions do you have regarding the cause of the accident in this case?

ANSWER: I believe that the accident was the result of metal fatigue, caused by poor maintenance.

QUESTION: Let's try to be a little more specific. What opinions do you have regarding the quality of maintenance?

The lawyer may continue to press the expert for continued statements of opinion, perhaps asking for the "factors," "considerations," or "elements" that make up the opinions.

In many jurisdictions an expert witness cannot provide an opinion at trial if it was not testified to at the deposition, so comprehensiveness tends to be in every party's best interest. As we have noted earlier, however, blanket answers can be misinterpreted, so it is usually desirable to avoid unqualified responses:

QUESTION: Are those all of your opinions in this case?

ANSWER: I suppose it might be possible to continue subdividing my opinions, but I think I have already told you about my major conclusions.

c. Bases for Opinions

Following the development of the expert's opinions, lawyers frequently inquire into the bases for the opinions. Taking the conclusions one at a time, the lawyer will ask,

QUESTION: What is the basis for your opinion that the plaintiff should have performed more frequent maintenance check-ups?

The witness's answer may come from the facts of the case, her research and testing, her knowledge of the area of practice, her experience in the particular field, or her professional judgment based on training and education.

Again, the lawyer may follow up by asking why a particular fact or test result supports the expert's opinion.

d. Assumptions

All experts must make assumptions, many of which are straightforward and will draw little attention during a deposition. For example, economic and financial experts will routinely assume that the United States Department of Labor accurately reports statistics on matters such as unemployment rates, labor efficiency, inflation, and cost-of-living variations.

Other assumptions involve the exercise of judgment and are therefore open to challenge, particularly when the expert has chosen among alternative possibilities. Looking again at a financial expert, imagine that the plaintiff's economist in the "restaurant" case projected lost profits for a period of ten years. The expert must then reduce the total damages to "present value" by using a discount rate based on a hypothesis about future interest rates. The choice of the discount rate, in turn, depends upon a number of smaller assumptions, each of which can be the subject of extended questioning at deposition.[10]

QUESTION: Dr. Lipton, what discount rate did you use in reducing your damage projection to present value?

QUESTION: Why did you choose that rate?

QUESTION: What data or statistics did you rely on in making your choice?

QUESTION: Were there other sources of data that you did not rely on, or that you rejected?

QUESTION: In preparing your opinion, did you perform your calculations using alternative discount rates?

---

10. A lower discount rate results in a higher estimate of current value; a higher rate means a lower damage calculation.

QUESTION: What was the result of looking at alternative discount rates?

QUESTION: How would your calculation change if you used a discount rate one-half point higher?

The lawyer may also choose to examine the expert on the limits or certainty of her assumptions:

QUESTION: Could a reasonable economist have chosen a higher discount rate?

QUESTION: Can you state with complete certainty that you have assumed the correct discount rate?

QUESTION: How might the actual discount rate differ from the one that you used in your assumptions?

QUESTION: Is there any way to tell whether actual interest rates in the future will be the same as the discount rate that you assumed?

QUESTION: Have you ever done a study to determine whether your own assumptions about discount rates have been borne out by actual interest rates over time?

e. Explanations

An attorney will frequently ask questions at deposition that he would never dream of asking on cross-examination: "Can you explain what you did? Why do you think that?" Those questions, and others like them, are deadly to the lawyer on cross-examination because they relinquish control to the witness. At deposition, however, the lawyer prefers information to control. By drawing out the full extent of the expert's reasons and explanations, the lawyer can limit the witness's testimony at trial and can better plan for cross-examination.

Consequently, a good part of every expert deposition is spent asking the witness to explain and expand upon every imaginable aspect of her preparation and opinion. The more the witness explains, the more likely she is either to contradict herself or to say something conceivably inconsistent with a previous publication.

f. Other Experts and Authorities

In trolling for information, lawyers will often use depositions to seek out or confirm other sources and authorities—for reasons either sincere or strategic. Some lawyers may truly want to know where to look for more information. They will ask the deponent for the names of additional experts, authors, books, resources, studies, and the like.

Somewhat more craftily, lawyers may also use the deposition to validate their own experts and sources. The request may be straightforward:

QUESTION: Dr. Lipton, are you aware that Dr. Isaacs has conducted a damage study that differs sharply from your own?

ANSWER: Yes, I have read Dr. Isaacs's report.

QUESTION: What is your opinion of Dr. Isaacs as an expert in the field of economic modeling?

The questioning may also be somewhat more obscure. Perhaps the lawyer has contacted several prospective experts but has not yet decided which one to retain. In that case, the deponent's advance opinion may be quite helpful in determining opposing counsel's choice:

QUESTION: Dr. Lipton, I am going to name six fairly prominent economists. Could you please rank them for me in terms of prominence in the field?

The same approach can be used with written authorities:

QUESTION: Dr. Lipton, could you please list the four most authoritative texts or sources in the field of economic modeling?

Or perhaps,

QUESTION: Dr. Lipton, assume that you had to answer an especially difficult and important question in your area of economic modeling. If you could consult only one book to help you find the answer, what would it be?

For fear of future cross-examination, it seems that some lawyers routinely advise experts never to concede that any other person (or book) can be called authoritative. This tactic can lead to absurd and potentially embarrassing results:

QUESTION: Dr. Lipton, can you name even one book or person that you consider authoritative in your field of economic modeling?

ANSWER: No. There are none.

Such a stubborn answer will probably do more harm on cross-examination than any concession the witness might possibly have made about "authoritativeness." Of course, the witness should still be attentive to traps and fallacies:

QUESTION: Dr. Lipton, do you consider the work of Professor Robert Burns to be authoritative in the field of economic damage modeling?

ANSWER: Professor Burns has done some very good work, but I could not say that he is authoritative on every issue.

g. Omissions

One crucial deposition question is whether the expert has any remaining work to do. A related inquiry is whether the expert, for whatever reason, omitted certain tests or steps in reaching her opinion. As noted with regard to cross-examination,[11] no matter how much the expert did, there will always be an infinite number of things she did not do. For each such "omission," the deposing lawyer may inquire at length. What didn't you do? What did you consider doing? Why didn't you do it? What results might you have seen? Who could you have talked to? What questions could you have asked? Why didn't you? Were you prevented from doing anything or talking to anyone?

F. Witness's Role—Coping with Counsel

A deposition witness must be truthful, forthright, candid, and cooperative. The trial process depends upon deponents to answer questions to the best of their ability so that cases can eventually be tried (or settled) on their merits. Expert witnesses are neither parties nor advocates, and it is not their job to camouflage their opinions or to obscure information.

None of this, however, prevents lawyers from baiting, harassing, intimidating, beguiling, or otherwise attempting to take advantage of expert witnesses. A witness who truly wants to give accurate testimony may nonetheless need to be cautious of counsel's finely honed techniques. The best advice, of course, is always to answer each question honestly and truthfully. Most experts will have questions about how to proceed in certain situations and how to avoid pitfalls and missteps.

---

11. Chapter Six, section H, *supra*.

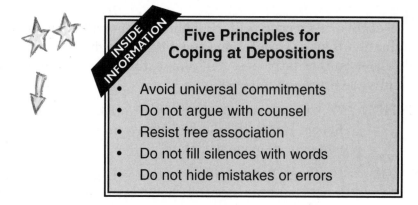

1. Questions and Answers

a. The Universal Commitment

It is a common deposition technique to draw a witness into stating her opinion in the form of a broad or universal assertion. Following such commitment, the attorney will reduce it to absurdity by applying it to new facts and circumstances. For example, assume that a medical expert has offered an opinion concerning sterilization procedures in a dental office:

QUESTION: Dr. Ascott, I gather it is your opinion that chemical sterilization of surgical instruments or supplies is never sufficient, correct?

ANSWER: Correct.

QUESTION: So it would be your opinion that no physician or dentist should ever utilize instruments or supplies that have not been heat sterilized in an autoclave, right?

ANSWER: Right.

QUESTION: Your opinion, then, would be based on that principle—that chemical sterilization is never appropriate?

ANSWER: That is my opinion.

On cross-examination at trial, or perhaps later in the deposition, the attorney will proceed to suggest a number of situations—emergencies, unusual circumstances, heat-sensitive materials—in which chemical sterilization may be completely appropriate, or at least not harmful or negligent. For example,

QUESTION: Dr. Ascott, are you familiar with a surgical procedure known as cricothyroidotomy?

ANSWER: I've heard of it.

QUESTION: Cricothyroidotomy is an emergency procedure for opening the windpipe, right?

ANSWER: I believe it is.

QUESTION: That procedure is almost never performed with heat-sterilized instruments, is it?

ANSWER: Probably not.

QUESTION: Are you familiar with the term "clean contaminated case"?

ANSWER: I am.

QUESTION: And that refers to a situation in which supplies are scrubbed clean, but not heat sterilized, correct?

ANSWER: Yes.

The witness has now been forced to concede that his original "principle" is not as ironclad as he claimed. The trap was laid when the expert was first led into overstating his opinion. Consider, then, a different initial answer:

QUESTION: Dr. Ascott, I gather it is your opinion that chemical sterilization of surgical instruments or supplies is never sufficient, correct?

ANSWER: My opinion is that chemical sterilization was insufficient in this case. There may be other circumstances where it is unavoidable.

When used in deposition questions, superlative words and phrases—never, always, must, best, greatest, foremost, or everything—are virtual signals that a qualified answer will be more accurate. In short, the old advice holds true: Never say never.

b. Arguing

It is not an expert witness's role to argue with the deposing attorney, or even to attempt to convince or educate the lawyer. First, the opposing lawyer can never be persuaded. It is not his job to be educated by the expert, but rather to locate the gaps or weaknesses in the expert's opinion. Second, jousting with a proficient lawyer is a contest that the deponent cannot win. The lawyer always gets to ask the final question. Even if the witness succeeds in concealing information or evading a question, the impression will be negative and therefore counterproductive:

QUESTION: Dr. Ascott, would it be your opinion that no physician or dentist should ever utilize instruments or supplies that have not been heat sterilized in an autoclave?

ANSWER: Well, "heat sterilized" is not the term I would use. Can you be more precise?

QUESTION: Would it ever be appropriate to rely on chemical sterilization?

ANSWER: That depends on what you mean by chemical sterilization.

QUESTION: Let me put it this way: Should all surgical instruments and supplies be sterilized in an autoclave?

ANSWER: That depends on what you mean by instruments and supplies.

A nimble witness can continue ad infinitum to challenge the lawyer's word choices or to search for tortured ambiguities. The lesson, however, is not that the witness has outsmarted lawyer. Rather, it is that the witness is slippery and therefore not to be trusted.

c. Free Association

There is an inclination among some experts to "think out loud" during a deposition, openly speculating or theorizing about possible alternative answers. This tendency can be encouraged by the deposing lawyer, since the witness's random thoughts may eventually include a gaffe or misstatement.

Sometimes a lawyer can successfully draw a witness into free association by doing nothing more than sitting silently across the deposition table. Because nature abhors a vacuum, the witness may be tempted to fill the silence by offering all sorts of unrequested testimony. This may well result in inaccuracy. Unbidden by any specific question, the volunteered information can be subject to misinterpretation or misconstruction.

d. Compulsion to Answer

No witness can answer every question. An expert should not be reluctant to say "I don't know" or "I don't remember" if that is the most accurate response.

Not every question can be readily answered. An expert should not be reluctant to say "I do not understand" if the question is ambiguous, vague, convoluted, or otherwise unanswerable.

e. Mistakes

Everyone makes mistakes, even the best-prepared expert witnesses. It is far worse to hide a mistake or to attempt to obscure it than it is to acknowledge and explain it.

2. Attire and Demeanor

Depositions are conducted outside the presence of judge and juror. In most cases, the only people present will be the witness, the court reporter, and the various attorneys. This can lead to a relatively relaxed and informal atmosphere. Unless the deposition is being held on the weekend, however, most (though not all) lawyers still wear business attire to depositions. Most witnesses also feel more comfortable and professional in business clothes, though there is no rule preventing more casual wear. Witnesses should be aware, however, that an increasing number of depositions are recorded on videotape and that the tapes may eventually be shown in court. In these circumstances, a witness should dress as she would for court.

However attired, a witness's demeanor at deposition should be professional and cooperative. The expert is there to play an important part in the litigation process, which calls for some considerable seriousness of purpose. Although the judge and jury are not present, every lawyer in the room will be evaluating the expert as a potential trial witness. Therefore, the disposition of the case may well be affected by the impression made by the expert witness.

Alas, we appear to live in an age of increasing incivility. It is not unknown for the lawyers in the deposition room to insult witnesses and to shout at one another (or vice versa). As unseemly as that may be among attorneys, it is even worse should the witness join the fray. A witness's best response to hostility is usually to take refuge in silence.

Finally, witnesses should be aware that the stenographic transcript does not indicate pauses in the testimony. A witness can pause and think for as long as she wishes after a question, and the transcript will read the same as though she had answered immediately. Videotape, however, makes pauses seem even longer.

G. Making the Record

Everything done at a deposition is done "for the record," since the very purpose of pretrial discovery is to create an account that can be later used for preparation or at trial. The following sections discuss some technical—and not so technical—aspects of making the record during a deposition.

1. Objections

Objections are a part of every deposition. Objections, to an attorney's question or the witness's answer, may be made for either of two reasons. The information sought may be inadmissible at trial, in which case the objection is made in order to "preserve" the issue until it can be ruled upon by a judge. Alternatively, the information sought may be "nondiscoverable," meaning that it does not have to be revealed by the deponent. Since some nondiscoverable information may be private, privileged, or sensitive, an objection on that basis may be accompanied by an instruction or request that the witness refrain from answering.

In the vast majority of situations an expert witness does not need to be concerned about the nature, basis, or validity of a lawyer's objections. It is nearly always sufficient for the witness to sit quietly until the lawyers have resolved the objection among themselves (remember, there is no judge). In the great majority of situations the witness will then be asked to answer the question "over the objection." The legal or evidentiary issues can be settled later, once the deposition has been completed.

In a few unusual circumstances one or more of the lawyers may decide that the deposition may not fairly proceed until an objection has been ruled upon by the court. When this happens the deposition may be recessed so that the attorneys may bring the question before a judge.

2. Instructions Not to Answer

Sometimes lawyers at depositions, intentionally or unintentionally, seek information that goes beyond the proper limits of discovery. They may ask about trade secrets, proprietary information, attorney-client communications, or other legally protected matters. In these circumstances the defending lawyer faces a dilemma. It is not sufficient to allow the question to be answered "over the objection" since the lawyer wants to protect the information from ever being revealed at all. Thus, the defending lawyer may "instruct the witness not to answer the question." By instructing a witness not to answer, the lawyer has taken the ultimate step to protect the requested information, insisting upon a court order before it will be disclosed.

As might be expected, a rather extensive body of case law has developed over the years regarding the circumstances under which a lawyer may instruct a witness to refrain from answering a deposition question. By and large, the parameter of the legal rule should not concern expert witnesses, since they will not be called upon to make legal judgments. There are two situations, however, in which an expert may have to decide on her own whether or not to answer a deposition question.

a. Instructions to Experts

There is some dispute over exactly which deponents may be instructed by a lawyer to refrain from answering deposition questions. Clearly, a lawyer may give such an instruction to his own client, since the purpose of the lawyer's presence at the deposition is to protect the client's legal rights. At the other extreme it seems equally evident that a lawyer may not "instruct" a bystander witness to refrain from answering. However impermissible the question, the attorney has no relationship with the third party that would allow him to give such a directive.

Expert witnesses fall somewhere in the middle. Obviously not a party to the suit or a client of the lawyer, the expert is nonetheless in a professional relationship with the lawyer and may have a separate obligation to protect confidential information. Some lawyers, however, take the position that it is improper to "instruct" an expert witness to refrain from answering questions. Consider the following truncated example:

DEPOSING
LAWYER: Mr. Expert, since you examined the plaintiff's payment accounts, please tell me the names of all of the plaintiff's best customers and special accounts.

DEFENDING
LAWYER: Objection. Counsel, that is proprietary information that is not subject to discovery. I am going to instruct the witness not to answer.

DEPOSING
LAWYER: The witness is not your client; you can't in-
           struct him. Mr. Expert, unless you are person-
           ally represented by the plaintiff's lawyer,
           please answer my question about the cus-
           tomer list.

What should the expert do? Accepting the instruction may appear to compromise his independence, but answering the question
might jeopardize confidential (and perhaps undiscoverable) information.

In this situation a little knowledge of the law becomes helpful.
Under the rules in virtually every jurisdiction, a party may protect
sensitive information from discovery by seeking a "protective order"
from the appropriate court.[12] Of course, a protective order would be
meaningless once the particular questions have been answered. Accordingly, a responsible expert can best respect the rights of all concerned by declining to answer the question at issue until every party
has had an opportunity to bring the issue before a judge. Return to
the "customer list" example:

DEPOSING
LAWYER: Mr. Witness, are you following counsel's in-
           struction not to answer my question?

EXPERT
WITNESS: I am choosing not to answer the question at
           this time, but not because of counsel's instruc-
           tion.

DEPOSING
LAWYER: On what basis are you refusing to answer my
           question?

EXPERT
WITNESS: An objection has been raised to the
           discoverability of that information. If I answer
           now, I will preclude counsel from seeking a
           protective order, which would not be fair. So I
           am temporarily declining to answer until all of
           the attorneys agree or until there has been a
           ruling by the court.

---

12. Rule 26(c), Federal Rules of Civil Procedure.

b. Protecting Other Clients

There is a second situation in which an expert may need to consider refusing to answer questions at a deposition. From time to time a lawyer may ask about other, unrelated cases on which the expert may have worked, perhaps to the point of intruding on confidences:

QUESTION: Dr. Gold, in your own practice have you ever treated patients suffering from acute, clinical depression?

ANSWER: Yes I have.

QUESTION: Did any of those patients manifest suicidal tendencies?

ANSWER: Several of them did.

QUESTION: Please tell me the name of every patient you ever treated who suffered from acute clinical depression and who manifested suicidal tendencies.

From the lawyers' perspective, this question calls for relevant information. The expert's treatment of similar patients may well be germane to her expert opinion in the current case. The retaining lawyer might not even object, since he might want to trumpet the extraordinary qualifications of his expert (or at least not appear to be hiding anything). After all, none of the current lawyers owe any duties to the expert's prior patients.

The expert, on the other hand, has an independent professional obligation to refrain from disclosing confidential information about other patients, whether or not there is an objection during the deposition. The expert can and should refuse to answer such a question and may need to consult personal counsel if the questioning persists.

3. "Off the Record"

The rules of procedure governing depositions require that all "testimony shall be taken stenographically or recorded by [another] method."[13] Questions and answers, therefore, must always be "on the record." From time to time, however, a lawyer may ask to go "off the record," meaning that the stenographer or videographer should temporarily stop recording. Strictly speaking, it requires the consent of every attorney in order to go off the record. Most lawyers, as a matter of courtesy, try to agree to reasonable requests.

---

13. Rule 30(c), Federal Rules of Civil Procedure.

Witnesses should be aware that, no matter what a lawyer says, nothing is actually off the record unless the court reporter stops writing or the recording device is turned off. Otherwise, whatever is recorded stays recorded, no matter what the witness understood as she was speaking.

a. Colloquy

Lawyers sometimes go off the record so that they can discuss things among themselves that do not need to be recorded. Transcript costs are usually figured by the page, so it can be wasteful and expensive to have the court reporter transcribe lengthy colloquies about procedural or scheduling issues.

Attorneys may also ask to go off the record in order to raise sensitive or potentially embarrassing matters, as in the following example:

DEPOSING
LAWYER: Could you please tell me where and when you initially spoke to Mr. Geraghty about whether you would be engaged as an expert in this case?

DEFENDING
LAWYER: Could we please go off the record?

DEPOSING
LAWYER: Certainly. Off the record. [Court reporter stops writing.]

DEFENDING
LAWYER: The witness and I actually first spoke about this case at a funeral. It was just a brief mention because the situation was very upsetting. I'd really appreciate it if you would skip to the first time we talked about the facts.

DEPOSING
LAWYER: No problem. Let's go back on the record. [Court reporter resumes writing.] Let me rephrase that last question; when was the first time you had a substantive discussion with Mr. Geraghty about the facts of this case?

b. Conferences

There is no uniform rule governing a witness's opportunity to confer with the retaining lawyer in the course of a deposition. Permissible practices vary from jurisdiction to jurisdiction and even from judge to judge.

Some lawyers insist that they have the "right" to confer with a witness at any time during the deposition, up to and including the time between a question and its answer. For the most part, however, no such right exists.[14] Lawyers who persist in interrupting deposition questions are abusing the process. Although it is not the witness's role to police the lawyers' conduct, no expert should allow an attorney to dictate her answers to deposition questions.

A more common rule is that lawyer and witness may confer only when "no question is pending." Thus, the witness must answer (or decline to answer) any pending question before she may go off the record to speak with retaining counsel.

Finally, a number of courts have moved to a far stricter approach, barring all off-record communication between retaining lawyer and witness during a deposition—with the single exception that conferences are permissible to discuss the possible assertion of a privilege. Thus, a witness may always ask to speak privately with retaining counsel if she believes that a question may call for privileged or other confidential information.

Off-record conferences may take several forms. The most casual approach involves whispered conversation at the deposition table. Of course, in these circumstances there is no guarantee that the other lawyers will not be able to hear everything being said. Indeed, the court reporter may even continue writing everything down unless there has been a clear agreement or instruction to go off the record. If a conference is truly for the purpose of discussing potentially confidential matters, it should probably be held away from the deposition table. In the most sensitive situations, the opposing set of lawyers and parties (and the court reporter) should be asked politely to leave the room.

c. Breaks

Depositions can be tiring, even grueling. A witness should not hesitate to ask for a short break or recess whenever it is needed.

---

14. The single exception, possible assertion of a privilege, is discussed later in this section.

H. Evidence Depositions

The previous sections of this chapter have focused on "discovery depositions," meaning depositions taken by the opposing party for the purpose of learning (or tying down) whatever the witness has to say.

An "evidence deposition," in contrast, is taken for the purpose of preserving the witness's testimony for use at trial. The witness may live in a foreign country or a distant state, or may be too ill to appear at trial. Thus, her testimony will be "preserved" by the deposition.

If an expert witness is likely to be unavailable for trial, retaining counsel may schedule an evidence deposition—probably on videotape. The evidence deposition will very much resemble trial testimony, with the retaining lawyer conducting a full direct examination, to be followed by the opposing attorney's cross-examination. Evidentiary objections will be made, though there will be no judge present to rule on them.

To be sure, excerpts of any deposition might eventually be offered as evidence at trial. In most jurisdictions the attorneys do not need to announce in advance whether the deposition is being taken for purposes of discovery or evidence. Retaining counsel, however, will surely know whether a particular deposition is intended to be used as a substitute for the witness's appearance at trial—in which case the witness will be expected to dress, act, and answer as though in the actual courtroom.

— Chapter Nine —

ETHICS AND PROFESSIONALISM

A. Introduction

The term "professional ethics" typically refers to the distinct, mandatory responsibilities undertaken by individuals in the course of practicing a trade or calling. Breaches of professional ethics may result in discipline, fee forfeiture, or other adverse consequences. In contrast, the term "professionalism" is often used to identify admirable, model, or ideal conduct that is generally expected—but not absolutely required.

For example, professional ethics compel a physician to maintain a patient's confidences; violating confidences may result in censure or worse. A sense of professionalism entails courtesy, clear communication, and punctuality; abandoning these standards may result in a loss of confidence or respect. The two concepts, of course, are not wholly distinct. Both are aspirational. Most professionals certainly do not adhere to ethical standards simply as a means of avoiding discipline or liability. Thus, this chapter discusses both professional ethics and professionalism.

Many professional obligations are identical to personal ethics or moral standards. Outright lying, for example, would commonly be understood as both a moral fault and a violation of professional standards. In many circumstances, however, professional ethics may be quite different from personal ethics. While most citizens believe it their duty to report crimes, lawyers usually must maintain confidences even when the clients have revealed serious criminal behavior. Conversely, physicians and social workers, among others, are expected to contact the authorities in cases of suspected child abuse, even in ambiguous situations where ordinary citizens might be justified in remaining uninvolved. The comparison of personal and professional ethics is sometimes referred to as "role differentiation," because ethical requirements vary according to the role one has assumed.

169

All expert witnesses are governed by personal ethics, and all must obey the rules of the courts in which they appear. But there is no single source that we can look to for a definitive statement of expert witness's professional ethics. A few organizations have attempted to draft codes of conduct for expert witnesses, but none have achieved broad acceptance.

As we have seen, experts may be drawn from virtually any field or calling, from aeronautics to zoology. In some cases the expert's own profession may have a well-developed code of ethics, as is the case in accounting, medicine, law, and psychotherapy. Such experts certainly must adhere to the standards of their own fields concerning matters such as confidentiality and conflicts of interest. They may even be subject to professional regulation or discipline for their conduct as witnesses.

Other professions are unlicensed or unregulated. A musician or composer, for example, might be called as a witness in a copyright case; economists are frequently called to testify in antitrust or tort cases. Neither profession has promulgated a code of ethics, and there are no generally recognized standards governing their conduct in forensic matters. The same is true of "human factors" experts, demographers, political scientists, penologists, journalists, and many others who are frequently called upon to testify in court.

The absence of an enacted code of conduct does not at all imply an absence of content-related professional standards. Academic and industrial scientists, for example, are expected to adhere to strict requirements of objectivity and to follow precise methods of investigation.

This chapter deals with the topic of "role differentiated" ethics for expert witnesses. It covers questions that may not arise, or that may arise differently, in the course of the expert's ordinary, nonforensic work. Specifically, we will address the issues of independence, confidentiality, conflicts of interest, fees, and conduct during trial and discovery.

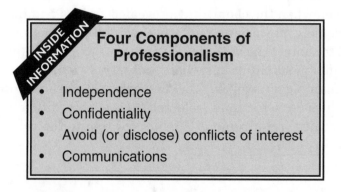

INSIDE INFORMATION

Four Components of Professionalism

- Independence
- Confidentiality
- Avoid (or disclose) conflicts of interest
- Communications

B. Independence and Objectivity

The single most important obligation of an expert witness is to approach every question with independence and objectivity. Recall that expert testimony is allowed only if the expert's "specialized knowledge will assist the trier of fact to understand the evidence."[1] The expert's opinion, in turn, cannot assist the fact finder's understanding unless that opinion is candidly and frankly based upon the witness's own investigation, research, and understanding.

An objective expert views the facts and data dispassionately, without regard to the consequences for the client. An independent expert is not affected by the goals of the party for which she was retained and is not reticent to arrive at an opinion that fails to support the client's legal position.

1. Coping with Lawyers

It will probably come as no surprise that there are lawyers who will attempt to influence the content of an expert's testimony. After all, advocates typically retain experts with one purpose in mind: to win the case. Given the effort and expense involved, some lawyers will be tempted to see the expert as simply another member of the litigation team. While expert witnesses will obviously have to work closely with the lawyers who engage them, it is important to maintain a sharp distinction between their roles.

As an advocate in the adversary system, it is a lawyer's job to make the best possible argument in support of her client. A lawyer will often find herself advancing a position in the hope that it will work, without necessarily believing that the view is correct. Lawyers do not testify under oath. While they must be truthful concerning facts and accurate in their representations about the content of the law, their opinions and arguments must always be adapted to the needs of their clients. In the classic formulation of the advocate's duty, Boswell reported that Dr. Johnson did not hesitate to raise arguments that he knew to be weak:

> Sir, you do not know it to be good or bad till the judge determines it. . . . An argument which does not convince yourself, may convince the judge to whom you urge it: And if it does convince him, why, then Sir, you are wrong and he is right.[2]

---

1. Rule 702, Federal Rules of Evidence.
2. 2 James Boswell, *The Life of Johnson* 47 (Hill Ed. 1887).

Experts, however, have no such latitude. As a witness, testifying under oath, you are not entitled to state a position "which does not convince yourself" in the hope that it may convince the judge or jury. The entire system of expert testimony rests upon the assumption that expert witnesses are independent of retaining counsel and that they testify sincerely.

Most lawyers understand and accept this on an intellectual level. Still, in the heat of adversary battle, it is not unknown for lawyers to seek, shall we say, to broaden or expand an expert's opinion in just the right direction. This is wrong. It is no more acceptable for a lawyer to push an expert into altering her opinion than it would be to convince an eyewitness to change his account of the facts.

2. Working with Lawyers

The need for independence and objectivity does not prevent experts from working closely with the lawyers who retain them. Litigation is a complex process, and it is important that attorneys be able to communicate with the experts working on the case. The lawyers will invariably have important information, and perhaps suggestions, that will facilitate the experts' work. They may also need constant input from the experts as the case proceeds, so that they may adjust their goals and strategies in light of the experts' findings.

It is entirely legitimate for expert witnesses to cooperate closely with retaining counsel, so long as the relationship remains independent and professional roles are not blurred.

a. Information and Assumptions

To one degree or another, all experts depend upon retaining counsel for the information necessary to do their work. At a minimum, the attorney will have to provide the expert with an explanation of the case, a description of the questions to be addressed by the expert, and the documents or other sources necessary to the expert's assignment. This will ordinarily be an interactive process, with the expert and the lawyer exchanging questions and information.

In many cases the lawyer will also have to inform the expert of the precise legal standard that must be addressed. Of course, some scientific or technical questions may seem purely descriptive: What is the composition of the chemical compound? What caused the stress fractures? What is the standard maintenance schedule for the part in question? But even in these situations, the expert may need to be aware of certain legal standards. For example, we saw in Chapter

One that the test for admissibility of an expert's opinion may vary from state to state. Thus, it is essential that the expert be aware of the relevant test as followed in the particular jurisdiction. This information can come only from retaining counsel. Moreover, it is certainly permissible for the expert to work with the attorney in order to make sure that the opinion is formed in a manner that will be admissible in court.

In other circumstances there may be legal rules that govern the necessary content of the expert's opinion. A psychologist, for example, would need to understand a jurisdiction's legal test for insanity or incompetence. An economist would have to know what items could properly be included in a damage study. Again, it is entirely proper for the expert to obtain direction on such matters from the attorneys on the case.

An expert's opinion will often be dependent or contingent upon facts that must be provided by other witnesses. Such facts may or may not be readily accessible, and they will sometimes be hotly disputed between the parties. Counsel may therefore ask the witness to "assume" certain facts, rather than have the witness undertake an independent investigation. This is an acceptable way to proceed, so long as the assumptions are reasonable and clearly identified.

Conversely, not every fact in a case will eventually be allowed into evidence at trial. A lawyer may therefore ask an expert to disregard certain information, on the theory that it is legally irrelevant or inadmissible. An expert may ethically comply with such a request, since the admissibility of evidence is not within the witness's purview.

For example, suppose that an economist has been retained by the defendant in a "wrongful discharge from employment" case. The expert's task is to determine the plaintiff's damages in the event that liability is established. Depending upon the jurisdiction, the elements of such a damage claim might possibly include back pay, future pay, and increments due to imputed promotions. A competent economist could calculate damages in all three categories, but would have no way of knowing which ones would be recognized by the court. Thus, the witness may rely on directions from counsel in determining which components to consider.

b. Suggestions and Questions

In addition to providing information and assumptions, a lawyer may also make suggestions or ask questions. When done properly, this is simply part of the intellectual exchange between two professionals. There may be evident gaps in the expert's analysis, or the reasoning may not clearly support the conclusions. The expert may not have adverted to all of the relevant factors. It is fair and appropriate for the lawyer to ask the expert to reconsider a conclusion in light of additional information. The retaining lawyer may ask pointed questions to make sure that the expert's position is thorough and valid. The attorney may suggest ways that the opinion could be strengthened or supported.

On the other hand, it is unacceptable for a lawyer to attempt to pressure a witness into changing or expanding her opinion. A lawyer must ultimately be willing to take the bad news with the good and to realize that the expert's opinion is unfavorable to (or not fully supportive of) the client's position.

A lawyer with integrity will normally accept a negative opinion, or even appreciate it, since that may help counsel and client formulate a settlement strategy rather than take a losing case to trial.

c. Trial Preparation

It is not unethical for a lawyer to assist an expert in preparing for trial or deposition. Counsel may inform the witness of the questions to be asked on direct examination and may alert the witness to potential cross-examination. The lawyer may describe the deposition process to the witness and caution the expert about the risks of volubility. Counsel may tell the witness if her answers seem confusing, unclear, or misleading, or if they are likely to be misinterpreted or misconstrued. An expert may be advised to use powerful language, to avoid jargon, to use analogies, to refrain from long narratives, or to use other means that will help her convey an opinion accurately.

Needless to say, the lawyer absolutely may not instruct a witness in how to testify.

d. Scope of Expertise

It is not unknown for an attorney to try to stretch a witness's expertise, either as a cost-saving measure or in an effort to broaden the impact of the testimony. For counsel, the engagement of expert witnesses can be time consuming and expensive, so there is somewhat of a natural impulse to see if the witness can do "double duty."

The situation is usually resolved simply by an appropriate inquiry. Either the witness is legitimately able to opine on the subject, in which case the engagement proceeds on that basis, or the witness lacks the necessary qualifications, in which case the subject is dropped.

More troubling is the possibility that some lawyers might try to induce or inveigle an expert to offer opinions that are truly beyond the scope of her expertise. Such testimony, if given, puts the witness out on a limb that may well be sawed off during cross-examination. Tactics aside, experts must be both qualified and independent. It is therefore unethical for a lawyer to tamper with the independence of an expert's views by attempting to persuade her to exaggerate her qualifications.

Honorable experts will not allow attorneys to overstate the scope of their opinions, and honorable counsel will respect this position.

C. Confidentiality

Professional obligations of confidentiality are well recognized. Lawyers, physicians, psychotherapists, clergy, and accountants all operate under various duties of secrecy. It is important for expert witnesses to understand that these duties generally do not apply in situations where they have been retained for the purpose of testifying in court.[3]

Notwithstanding the usually privileged nature of their communications, expert witnesses may be expected, and even compelled, to reveal conversations that would otherwise be inviolate. The reason for this distinction should be obvious. Evaluation and testimony do not fall within the ordinary practice of a profession. Communications made to a retained witness, for the very purpose of providing testimony in court, do not fall within the "zone of privacy" necessary for the invocation of an evidentiary privilege. Of course, many professionals—engineers, architects, economists, chemists, and others—do not ordinarily enjoy a privilege of confidentiality.

Consequently, expert witnesses should assume that all of their communications, with either the client or retaining counsel, may be subject to disclosure through the process of discovery. Additionally, the witness's research files, work papers, notes, drafts, correspondence, and similar materials may have to be revealed to the attorneys for opposing parties. In some jurisdictions it is possible that some items may be protected from discovery, but prudence dictates that the witness presume that her file will be an open book.

---

3. Even where the witness was not retained for the purpose of testimony, as in the case of a treating physician, most professional privileges are waived once the witness is called to testify.

This is not to say, however, that the expert has no obligations of confidentiality to the client. Even in the absence of a separate ethical duty, principles of agency law require that an expert take reasonable steps to safeguard client confidences and refrain from using confidential information for self-enrichment or other improper purposes.[4]

One recurrent issue involves the efforts of lawyers to contact opposing expert witnesses outside the processes of formal discovery. Many courts have held that access to experts is limited by the discovery rules and that all interviews must take place via deposition. In a few jurisdictions, however, extramural interviews have been found permissible. But even in jurisdictions where the lawyer is permitted to contact the expert, there is no obligation that the expert respond. Most experts would consider it unprofessional, at the very least, to hold ex parte discussions with opposing counsel in the absence of notice to the retaining lawyer. At the extreme, unauthorized contact with an adverse party's expert may be considered witness tampering, perhaps leading to disqualification of the lawyer or witness, or other sanctions.[5]

Because of the complex interplay among professional ethics standards, rules of evidence, discovery, and other law, it is best to clarify expectations of confidentiality at the outset of every engagement. According to the American Bar Association Standing Committee on Professional Conduct, a retention letter "should define the relationship, including its scope and limitations, and should outline the responsibilities of the testifying expert, especially regarding the disclosure of client confidences."[6]

D. Loyalty and Conflicts of Interest

For expert witnesses, issues of loyalty and conflicts of interest raise two different questions: (1) If the matters are unrelated, may a witness accept concurrent engagements both for and against the same party (or law firm)? (2) May an expert "switch sides" in litigation?

---

4. Other law may also limit the expert's use of confidential information. For example, an economic expert may obtain "insider information" concerning a publicly traded corporation. The use of this information for investment purposes could constitute a crime under the federal Securities Exchange Act.

5. See, e.g., *Erickson v. Newmar Corp.*, 87 F. 3d 298 (9th Cir. 1996).

6. American Bar Association Standing Committee on Professional Conduct, Formal Opinion 97-407 (May 13, 1997).

1. Unrelated Engagements

It is a well-established rule of legal ethics that a lawyer may not engage in representation "directly adverse" to a current client. Thus, even in completely unrelated cases, a lawyer may not simultaneously sue and defend the same party.[7] This rule is based upon the principle of attorney loyalty, which must never be diluted by undertaking obligations to adverse parties.

Expert witnesses, on the other, do not owe that sort of loyalty to their clients. An expert is not the client's "champion," pledged faithfully to seek the client's goals. Indeed, in many ways the expert's role is precisely the opposite. She must remain independent of the client and detached, if not wholly aloof, from the client's goals.[8]

There is no reason that an objective expert could not conclude—and explain—that a party is correct in one case and wrong in another. Consequently, there is no general ethical principle that prevents an expert from accepting concurrent engagements both for and adverse to the same party.[9]

By the same token, it follows that an expert may simultaneously work with and against a lawyer or law firm, testifying for the law firm's client in one case and against the firm in another. Finally, since there is no rule against accepting concurrent adverse engagements, there is also no general restriction on testifying adversely to a former client or against a law firm by which one was previously retained.

The expert's freedom of action, however, is not absolute. As noted in the previous section, the law of agency imposes an obligation to refrain from exploiting a client's confidences for the benefit of another. Thus, an expert should not accept conflicting engagements, either concurrently or successively, that are factually related, since this could risk misuse or exploitation of a client's confidences.[10]

There is a further constraint on the acceptance of engagements, though it is difficult to quantify. It will surely cause a law firm or client great discomfort to see his expert turn up on the opposite side of another lawsuit. Though the matters may be unrelated, with no

---

7. American Bar Association Model Rules of Professional Conduct, Rule 1.7(a). The lawyer may engage in such representation if the clients consent following disclosure.

8. "A duty to advance a client's objectives diligently through all lawful measures, which is inherent in a client-lawyer relationship, is inconsistent with the duty of a testifying expert." American Bar Association Standing Committee on Professional Conduct, Formal Opinion 97-407 (May 13, 1997).

9. In fact, there is authority that one person may testify for both sides (on different issues) in the same lawsuit.

10. Of course, the affected client could consent.

threat to client confidences, the expert's dual position obviously places counsel in the troublesome position of having to extoll the expert's opinion in one case while attacking it in another. Needless to say, most lawyers would find this situation either damaging to the expert's credibility in case one or damaging to the client's position in case two (or both). No doubt, the retaining lawyer would prefer to avoid this dilemma if possible, even if there is no ethical bar to the expert's actions.

As a matter of courtesy and professionalism, it is best to resolve this issue at the outset of every case. A lawyer may request that the expert refrain from accepting potentially adverse engagements, at least for the duration of the retention. The expert may accept or decline the proposed restriction, or may suggest other terms. The absence of an ethics rule does not prevent the attorney and expert from negotiating a mutually agreeable resolution to what could perhaps become a sticky problem. In any event, forthright discussion of terms and conditions can prevent the development of an awkward situation down the road.

2. Switching Sides

Imagine that an expert has been retained by the plaintiff in a lawsuit. The expert conducts her research and arrives at an opinion that is quite unfavorable to the plaintiff, who then discharges the witness. May the witness subsequently testify for the defendant, whose position is supported by the expert's work?

There is no per se rule that prohibits an expert witness from switching sides in a lawsuit. Since the expert's job is to arrive at an independent opinion, it cannot be disloyal for the witness to begin working for one party and end up working for the other. On a case-by-case basis, however, considerations of confidentiality and privilege will often operate to prevent an expert from switching sides.

The answer to the question will ultimately depend upon the nature and extent of the relationship between the expert and the original client. In brief, an expert may not switch sides, even following discharge or release, if that would violate the client's reasonable expectation of confidentiality. This in turn will depend on a number of factors. How extensive was the communication between the expert and the client (or the client's counsel)? Was the expert provided nonpublic or privileged information? Did the expert participate in strategy discussions with counsel, or otherwise learn of the client's decision-making strategy?

While the courts have used a variety of tests to weigh these factors, it is fair to say that the touchstone has invariably been access to confidential information. Hence, an expert who only participated in a short preliminary discussion with one attorney would be free to accept retention from the other side. Conversely, an expert who had performed an extensive fact investigation, working closely with counsel, would likely be barred from switching sides.

A further distinction should be made between a witness who is discharged (or who initially declined an engagement) and a witness who defects. There are few cases dealing with the latter phenomenon, no doubt because it seldom occurs. Nonetheless, a witness who deliberately sets out to switch sides, or who is lured away by opposing counsel, may well find herself disqualified from testifying in the case. Not only is such a witness likely to have compromised confidences, but a defecting witness also creates the appearance of chicanery. A court may bar the witness on the ground that her conduct (or counsel's) has been "prejudicial to the administration of justice."

Again, most difficulties can be avoided if there is frank discussion at the outset of the engagement. A well-drafted retention letter will spell out the expert's duties and the client's expectations concerning confidential information, as well as the expert's options in the event of discharge or release.[11]

E. Fees

Unlike other witnesses who can be reimbursed only for expenses, an expert may be paid a fee for preparing and testifying in court.[12] A variety of ethics issues arise in the context of expert's possible fee arrangements.

1. Contingency Fees

It is considered unethical in virtually every jurisdiction to pay an expert witness a contingency fee,[13] meaning a fee that is "contingent upon the content of [the] testimony or the outcome of the case."[14]

---

11. Concerning the relationship between preclusion and fee arrangements, see section E.3, *infra*.

12. American Bar Association Model Rules of Professional Conduct, Rule 3.4(b) comment. See also, American Bar Association Model Code of Professional Conduct, DR 7-109(C).

13. American Bar Association Model Rules of Professional Conduct, Rule 3.4(b) comment. See also, American Bar Association Model Code of Professional Conduct, DR 7-109(C).

14. The quoted language is from the American Bar Association Model Code of Professional Conduct, DR 7-109(C). The Model Code has been superseded in most states by the Model Rules of Professional Conduct, but the definitions of "contingent fee" remains accurate. See, e.g., Rule 3.3(a)(15), Illinois Rules of Professional Conduct.

Such fees are prohibited because they create an unacceptable incentive for the expert to tailor her opinion to the needs or interests of the retaining party. In other words, the expert's independence and objectivity become impaired when payment hinges on the success of the litigation.

A similar, though not identical, problem may be raised by other fee structures. Consider, for example, the practice of "value billing," which has increasingly been used by lawyers and consultants. In value billing, the fee is eventually determined by the value or benefit conferred by the work, rather than by the number of hours devoted to the task. For expert witnesses, however, value billing can come uncomfortably close to charging on the basis of "the content of the testimony."

For example, imagine that an expert follows a policy of rebating or returning fees in the event that her opinion cannot be used by the retaining party. While the expert might justify this approach as an effort to avoid excessive billing for unproductive work, it clearly results in additional compensation when the expert's opinion is favorable to the client. The same result occurs when the expert's hourly rate is adjusted (up or down) following the initial research or evaluation.

In order to avoid any suggestion of "contingency," most experts bill at a constant hourly rate.[15] Of course, even in these circumstances a favorable initial evaluation may presumably lead to further hours spent on preparation, deposition, and perhaps trial testimony. While this additional work will obviously result in greater total compensation, it is not considered a contingent fee.

2. Flat Fees, Minimums, and Advances

In addition to hourly billing, other fee structures may include or combine flat fees, minimums, or retainers. Unless they are excessive, none of these devices present ethical problems.

A flat fee compensates the expert in a set amount for all, or some defined portion, of the work. For example, a flat fee could cover the entire engagement all the way through testimony at trial, or it could be determined in stages—perhaps one amount for the initial research and work-up, another if a written report becomes necessary, and a final amount for deposition and trial time.

---

15. Some experts bill at a higher (or "premium") rate for time spent in deposition or trial, on the theory that such time is more taxing or arduous. In the same vein, many lawyers charge more for trial time and physicians charge more for surgery than they do for office visits. "Premium time" billing is not regarded as unethical, though the practice is not widespread.

A minimum fee, usually used in conjunction with an hourly rate, ensures that the expert will be compensated at a certain level regardless of the amount of work ultimately involved in the case. An advance, sometimes also called a retainer, provides the witness with some or all of her payment at the outset of the engagement, rather than billing exclusively as work is performed.

To one degree or another, each of these fee structures provides additional security to the expert. In that sense, minimums, flat fees, and advances may be seen as the "flip side" of contingent fees. In each case, guaranteed payment becomes entirely disengaged from the content of the expert's opinion.

3. Lock-up Fees

Some expert witnesses insist upon the payment of a nonrefundable "lock-up" fee at the outset of every engagement. The amount may be small or large, but in either case the purpose of the fee is to compensate the witness for agreeing to forego retention by the other parties in the litigation.

As noted in an earlier section, an expert who has received significant confidences from one party may not thereafter accept retention by the other side. Thus, there is some financial risk, especially in the case of a prominent individual, whenever an expert agrees to begin working on a case. It may be only a few hours until the expert reaches an opinion adverse to the retaining client, yet the expert might then be precluded from doing further work (and billing additional hours) for another party in the litigation. The lock-up fee resolves this dilemma by, in essence, providing the expert with a "signing bonus" in exchange for agreeing to work exclusively with one client in the matter.

When used by lawyers, particularly in criminal and divorce cases, the nonrefundable retainer has been criticized as oppressive and exploitive.[16] A number of jurisdictions have either banned or sharply curtailed their use by attorneys.[17]

In this regard, however, expert witnesses do not operate under the same restraints as lawyers. The chief objection to the attorney's nonrefundable retainer is that the forfeiture of the retainer creates a de facto impediment to firing the lawyer. In turn, this chills the client's unfettered right to discharge counsel at any time

16. Lester Brickman & Lawrence Cunningham, "Nonrefundable Retainers: Impermissible Under Fiduciary, Statutory and Contract Law," 57 *Fordham Law Review* 149 (1988).
17. See, e.g., *In re Cooperman*, 633 N.E.2d 1069 (N.Y. 1994).

without cost or penalty. But the same considerations do not apply to experts. To be sure, the client is always free to fire an expert witness, but no comparable public policy is served by ensuring that there is no financial loss to the client who does so.[18]

Lock-up fees should not be considered unethical when used by expert witnesses.

F. Discovery

Discovery, as discussed in Chapter Eight, is the formal process in which lawyers are able to gain facts and information about the opposing party's case. As applied to expert witnesses, the forms and details of discovery are addressed in the preceding chapter. Ethics issues also arise in the discovery process.

1. Communicating with Adverse Counsel

The Federal Rules of Civil Procedure, and the corresponding provisions in most states, place limits on the right of one lawyer to contact opposing counsel's experts. In brief, experts are divided into two categories: Those who have been identified as "testifying experts," and those who have been consulted but who have not (or not yet) been listed as witnesses. The latter group of experts are sometimes called either "consulting experts" or "non-testifying experts." Although there are limited exceptions, only testifying experts are broadly subject to discovery. Purely consulting experts, other than in extreme circumstances, are exempt from discovery.[19]

As we saw above,[20] an enterprising lawyer may occasionally seek an extracurricular interview with the opposing party's expert. Although the courts are somewhat divided on the propriety of this tactic, the majority view is that such contacts are prohibited in the case of both testifying and non-testifying experts.

While the discovery rules probably do not constrain the witnesses themselves, agency principles require reasonable steps to maintain a client's confidences. A responsible expert, therefore, should notify

---

18. For an extended discussion of the use of nonrefundable retainers by certain expert witnesses, see Lester Brickman & Lawrence Cunningham, "Nonrefundable Retainers Revisited," 72 *North Carolina Law Review* 1 (1993) (arguing against use of nonrefundable retainers by lawyer "ethics experts"); Steven Lubet, "The Rush to Remedies: Some Conceptual Questions About Nonrefundable Retainers," 73 *North Carolina Law Review* 271 (1994) (arguing that use of nonrefundable retainers by expert witnesses is ethically acceptable); Lester Brickman & Lawrence Cunningham, "Nonrefundable Retainers: A Response to Critics of the Absolute Ban," 64 *University of Cincinnati Law Review* 11 (1995) (relenting).

19. Rule 26(b)(4), Federal Rules of Civil Procedure.

20. See section C, *supra*.

retaining counsel in the event she is approached for substantive information by an attorney for an adverse party.

2. Production of Documents

A testifying expert's entire file will usually be subject to full disclosure to the adverse party. On the other hand, a non-testifying expert's materials are discoverable only under very unusual circumstances. Discoverability is a legal question to be resolved by the lawyers and court. Experts are not expected to decide on their own which materials should and should not be disclosed.

Discovery requests to experts are channeled through retaining counsel. Typically, the attorney will ask the expert for a described set of materials (perhaps "everything"), and the expert will either copy them or turn over the originals. The lawyer will then decide which items must be produced to the other side. In some situations, especially in criminal cases, the material may be sought directly from the witness via subpoena.

It is unethical, and perhaps even criminal, to conceal or destroy material that has been subpoenaed or requested in discovery. Of course, disclosure may be resisted. There can be objections to discovery, and subpoenas may be quashed. But that process nonetheless requires good faith compliance, or at least acknowledgment of the existence of the requested items.

An expert may ordinarily rely upon the decisions of retaining counsel with regard to discoverability. It is not unusual for a lawyer to advise a witness that certain documents must be produced while others need not be. In either case, however, the witness must forthrightly answer questions about the existence and location of documents or physical objects relevant to the expert's work.

Most important, an expert should never destroy any item—document, object, photograph, record—for the purpose of concealing it from discovery or obstructing another party's access to evidence. Of course, papers and objects may be discarded in the ordinary course of "housekeeping," but any item that has been requested in discovery must be preserved until the request has been complied with by the expert or disallowed by a court.

3. Depositions

A deposition is pretrial testimony, taken under oath for the purpose of discovering what the witness has to say. Depositions generally proceed in a lawyer's office. There is no judge present, and consequently there is no one there to resolve disputes between the attorneys or to instruct the witness how to proceed. There are relatively few ethical problems exclusive to depositions, though all of the standard issues—confidentiality, coaching, candor—certainly can and do arise. In addition, the fact that no judge is present during the testimony raises one unique question.

From time to time in the course of almost every deposition, lawyers are inclined to confer with their witnesses. Sometimes the conference occurs "off the record," either in whispers at the table or during a formal recess. Other times the lawyer speaks directly to the witness "on the record," with all counsel present and the court reporter busily transcribing everyone's remarks. On-record comments often come in the form of instructions or advice to the witness. Either circumstance can quickly become uncomfortable for an expert, especially if the witness is unfamiliar with local procedures.

a. Conferring Off the Record

Jurisdictions differ widely, one is tempted to say wildly, about the acceptability of conferences between lawyer and witness in the course of a deposition. It was once considered routine almost everywhere for lawyers to pull aside their witnesses so long as there was no question pending at that particular moment. While most such conferences were no doubt conducted in good faith—to clarify a point, to preserve a confidence, to calm down a nervous witness—they were also the occasion of much abuse. Too many lawyers used off-record conferences to obstruct the deposition, coach the witness, or worse.

In a predictable reaction, courts in many jurisdictions have now issued rules or orders that significantly limit a lawyer's right to confer with a witness during deposition. The most drastic restrictions prohibit all conferences, other than those necessary to determine the applicability of an evidentiary privilege.[21]

Though the clear trend is toward the regulation, if not outright elimination, of witness conferences, it has not taken hold everywhere. Consequently, expert witnesses may face a great variety of environments and may not always be able to count on the lawyers for clear or knowledgeable directions. What is a witness to do?

The rules of deposition procedure are aimed primarily at counsel, and lawyers are expected to understand and follow the rules. Consequently, experts may generally rely on counsel's representations

---

21. Concerning the invocation of privilege at depositions, see Section F.3.b, *infra.*

concerning the acceptability of off-record conferences. Certainly, if the deposing lawyer does not object, the witness has little reason to be concerned about the propriety of the conference.

On the other hand, the deposing lawyer may well object. The following scenario places the witness in an extremely awkward position

RETAINING
LAWYER: Excuse me, but I need to confer with the witness for a moment before you ask the next question. Let's go off the record.

DEPOSING
LAWYER: Off-record conferences are not permitted in this jurisdiction, especially with expert witnesses. Let's proceed.

RETAINING
LAWYER: You're wrong about that. We're going off the record.

DEPOSING
LAWYER: I object. If you insist on conferring off the record you will be putting yourself—and the witness—at risk of contempt of court. I will seek a protective order, and I intend to enforce it.

RETAINING
LAWYER: I'm taking my witness out of the room. I'll tell you when we are ready to reconvene. [Speaking to the witness] Let's get out of here.

It is not the witness's job to resolve this squabble between the attorneys. While there must be an answer to the controversy—the conference is either allowed or it is not—the witness ordinarily has no way of knowing which lawyer is correct.

Unless the witness has reliable independent knowledge of the jurisdiction's rule, the best approach to this problem is probably to follow the directions of the retaining lawyer. Recall that an expert has specific professional obligations to the client, including a duty to take reasonable steps to protect certain confidences. It is the retaining lawyer who speaks for the client, and it is the retaining lawyer who is most knowledgeable about the effect of the deposition upon the client's confidences. Hence, the safer path is usually to accept the retaining lawyer's understanding of the rules.

* Nonetheless, experts should be aware that retaining counsel is not infallible. An expert should never—repeat never—violate or disregard a court order, no matter how many assurances are forthcoming from retaining counsel. Even where conferencing is freely allowed, an expert should likewise never permit retaining counsel to dictate or alter the content of her testimony. In extreme or extraordinary circumstances, the expert should consider whether she needs to consult her own attorney.

b. Instructions or Directions

From time to time, retaining counsel may interrupt a deposition by giving instructions directly to the witness. For example, if the lawyer believes that a particular question is improper or that it seeks privileged information, the witness will often be directed not to answer it. Such instructions generally occur on the record, often attended by spirited argument between the lawyers. The following colloquy is typical, including the ultimate challenge to the witness:

RETAINING
LAWYER: I object to that question since it calls for "work product." I instruct the witness not to answer.

DEPOSING
LAWYER: You waived work product when you designated the witness as a testifying expert. The question stands.

RETAINING
LAWYER: You can ask what you want, but the witness is not going to respond. If you want an answer, you'll have to take it before the judge.

DEPOSING
LAWYER: This witness is not your client. You can object, but you cannot give her any instructions. I am going to ask the question one more time. If the witness refuses to answer we will have no choice but to certify the question and get a court order compelling her to answer. [Speaking to the witness] Are you going to follow your lawyer's instructions and refuse to answer my question?

The witness is now in a bind. Retaining counsel has instructed her not to answer a question, but the deposing lawyer insists—threatening court action if she refuses. Which lawyer is right?

Which one should the witness believe? Most important, how should the witness respond?

As is often the case, it turns out that each lawyer is partially correct, and each is partially wrong. It is imperative that the retaining lawyer take the necessary steps to protect privileged information, including so-called work product.[22] Those steps may well include preventing an expert witness from disclosing otherwise undiscoverable information during a deposition. The deposing lawyer is accurate, however, in pointing out that the retaining lawyer does not represent the witness and cannot give her instructions. Although this might seem to confuse the matter, it actually suggests a clear course of conduct for the expert.

The witness must always be sensitive to the need to shield privileged information. Be aware that once information has been revealed, it may lose its protected nature even if the deposing lawyer was never entitled to it in the first place. This "cat out of the bag" rule requires extreme caution in responding to questions that have drawn objections. And while it is true that retaining counsel cannot instruct an expert to refrain from answering, that does not mean that the witness must answer.

Here is the solution. If the witness improperly declines to answer, the information can always be provided later. Thus, there is relatively little harm in refusing to answer a particular question, pending resolution by the lawyers or a ruling by the court. On the other hand, information can never be retrieved once it has been disclosed. Thus, great damage can be done by ignoring an objection and proceeding to reply.

In the absence of other factors, the best approach for a witness is to decline to answer questions once retaining counsel has objected on the basis of privilege or confidentiality.[23] A polite refusal to answer will preserve the objection so that it may, if necessary, be brought before the court. Hence,

DEPOSING
LAWYER: Are you going to follow your lawyer's instructions and refuse to answer my question?

---

22. An attorney's work product, including documents and tangible things "prepared in anticipation of litigation or for trial," is generally protected from discovery by the opposing party. Rule 26(b)(3), Federal Rules of Civil Procedure.

23. Not all objections require refusal to answer. Lawyers will often say something on the order of "Objection, the witness may answer." Experts need not concern themselves with the rules of evidence or other procedural complexities that create this situation.

EXPERT
WITNESS: I am not following anyone's instructions, but I decline to answer that question. It is not my job to resolve disputes between counsel about privilege or discoverability.

One last point. Note that the deposing attorney made a reference to "your lawyer's instruction." Retaining counsel is not the witness's lawyer. Expert witnesses are almost never represented by counsel at a deposition. The expert is there to provide an independent analysis and opinion. Since the expert is not a party to the case, the expert is not represented by either of the attorneys.

G. Trial Conduct

As with discovery, the basic principles of professional ethics govern an expert witness's conduct in trial. In addition, the expert must be aware of the following trial specific issues.

1. Ex Parte Communication

a. Judges

Ex parte communications are those that involve fewer than all of the parties who are legally entitled to be present during the discussion of any matter. During trial, it is normally prohibited for the judge to participate in a conversation that includes only one side of the case. Of course, the judge can engage in pleasantries with a single lawyer, and certain matters may legitimately be heard without all parties present.[24] But on matters related to the case at hand, the general rule is that all communication with the court must take place in the presence of all attorneys.

Thus, expert witnesses should not engage in private conversations with the court. Should the expert incidentally come in contact with the judge, perhaps in the hall or away from the courthouse entirely, care should be taken not to discuss the substance of the case or the content of the witness's testimony.

It occasionally occurs that an ex parte interview between the court and a witness is either authorized by law or agreed to by the parties. In those circumstances, of course, the witness may (and should) communicate candidly with the judge.

---

24. The legality of ex parte proceedings is beyond the scope of this book.

Unfortunately, it also occurs that judges seek out witnesses even without legal justification. Perhaps the judge is curious, incautious, or simply unaware of the extent of the rule against ex parte communication. Whatever the reason, such contact can obviously cause much discomfort for the witness. Most witnesses would never presume to question the judge's knowledge of law or ethics. And, of course, the judge is the judge—perhaps the interview is permitted under the circumstances of the case.

Unless the circumstances are clearly improper, it is reasonable for an expert witness to accede to a judge's request for a private interview. In all situations, however, the occurrence of such an interview should immediately be reported to all counsel in the case.

b. Jurors

All communication between an expert witness and the jurors must take place from the witness stand. It is never permissible for a witness to engage in private discussion with a juror. When encountering jurors in the courthouse hallway or cafeteria, contact should be limited to a polite smile or greeting. Under no circumstances should a witness ever discuss a case with a sitting juror.

2. Third-Party Communication

Once a trial has begun, and particularly after the witness has taken the stand, there are significant limits on the propriety of a witness's communications with others.

a. Other Witnesses

Many courts follow a policy of excluding witnesses from the courtroom while other witnesses are testifying. Experts are often excepted from such orders, but that is not always the case. Thus, an expert witness should always check with retaining counsel before attending the trial as an observer.

Equally important, experts must understand that the exclusion of witnesses is meant to prevent them from gaining knowledge of other witnesses' testimony; it is not merely a prohibition against sitting in the courtroom. Thus, an expert should not debrief another witness who has already testified and should not read the transcript of earlier testimony, other than at the direction of trial counsel.

b. Counsel

Once a witness has taken the stand, what matters may she discuss with retaining counsel during breaks and recesses? There is no single answer to this question, as the rules vary considerably from jurisdiction to jurisdiction.

In some courts it is considered improper for a witness who has already taken the stand to have any contact whatsoever with any of the attorneys. In other jurisdictions witnesses may speak with counsel, but not about the substance of the case. In yet other jurisdictions the witness and lawyer may speak freely, but the content of any discussion may be explored on cross-examination.

Complicating matters further, there is no unanimity as to when the various restrictions begin to apply. Thus, some states allow continuing lawyer-witness contact until the end of the direct examination, barring contact only once the witness has been "tendered for cross." In other courts the ban on communication begins as soon as the witness is placed under oath.

Needless to say, expert witnesses should determine the applicable rule for the court in question. Whatever the rule, the witness should comply.

c. The Press

In the absence of a gag order or secrecy statute, witnesses are free to speak with the press about the trials in which they have participated.

A sense of professionalism, however, counsels self-restraint. Ordinarily, a party to litigation does not retain an expert for the purpose of speaking to the press. The client may not want the case publicized and may not want to risk the exposure of confidences. In this regard, experts should take their cue from retaining counsel.

3. Excluded Evidence

With or without the expert's knowledge, certain evidence may have been ruled inadmissible by the court. Although judges most often make evidentiary rulings in response to objections at trial, they may also rule on motions in limine before the expert ever takes the stand.

Once evidence has been ruled inadmissible, either during or before the witness's testimony, it is unethical to sneak it in through the back door. Thus, if an expert has been instructed to refrain from testifying about certain facts or on certain issues, the witness should not attempt to blurt out the proscribed information on the pretext of answering an unrelated question.

Index

advance, 181
flat fee, 180
lock-up fee, 181-182
minimum fee, 181
Expert's report
format, 46
organization, 47-49
required content, 41, 47

F

Federal Rules of Civil Procedure
Rule 26(a)(2), 41
Rule 26(b)(1), 135
Rule 26(b)(3), 135, 187
Rule 26(b)(4), 182
Rule 26(c), 164
Rule 28(a), 139
Rule 30(c), 165
Rule 30(e), 140
Rule 36, 43
Federal Rules of Evidence
Rule 106, 114
Rule 610, 75
Rule 702, 3, 4, 53, 96, 171
Rule 703, 7
Rule 704(b), 5
Rule 705, 6, 56
Rule 803(18), 102, 127
Fees, 105, 133, 152, 179
Fluency, 21

I

Impeachment, 103-104, 112-113, 125
Information transfer, 33, 43, 44

Instructions not to answer, 162, 163, 186-187
Internal summaries, 70
Interrogatories, 40, 41, 137-138
Issue identification, 32-33

J

Jargon, 26, 66
Judicial admissions, 43

K

Knowledge bias, 20

L

Language, effective, 21-22
conversational manner, 26
plain speech, 65-67
strong wording, 70-71
Lay witnesses, 2
Learned treatise, 102-103, 127-128

N

Narratives, 67-69
Non-testifying experts, 135, 182

O

Objections
during direct examination, 75-77
during discovery depositions, 162
role of, 74
types of, 74
Off-the-stand behavior, 30